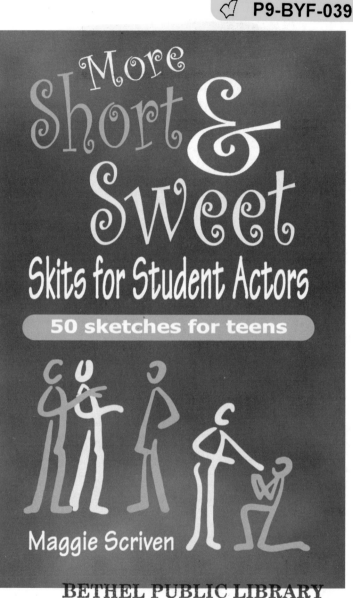

More Short & Sweet

Skits for Student Actors

50 sketches for teens

Maggie Scriven

mp

MERIWETHER PUBLISHING LTD.
Colorado Springs, Colorado

Meriwether Publishing Ltd., Publisher
PO Box 7710
Colorado Springs, CO 80933-7710

www.meriwether.com

Editor: Theodore O. Zapel
Assistant editor: Amy Hammelev
Cover design: Jan Melvin

Library of Congress Cataloging-in-Publication Data

Scriven, Maggie.
  More short & sweet skits for student actors : fifty sketches for teens / by Maggie Scriven. -- 1st ed.
      p. cm.
   ISBN 978-1-56608-185-6
1. Young adult drama, American. 2. Teenagers--Drama. I. Title. II. Title: More short and sweet skits for student actors.
  PS3619.C7565S24 2012
  812'.6--dc23

                                                            2011044863

    1   2   3   11   12   13

Dedicated to my best friend,
Debbie, who always had great ideas and
has been with me through thick and thin.

Explanation of the Résumé Elements

The above résumé is a very simple example of what most student actors can claim. It is very important that no one ever lie or exaggerate on a résumé; they will be found out and it won't go well for them! Don't hesitate, however, to have them include every performance, big and small, in which they have worked. Everything counts!

- *Name and address:* If a child is under age, he or she should use a parent as the point of contact. Include parent/guardian's name next to the phone number.

- *Stats:* Some very complex résumés will include clothing sizes and body measurements. This is particularly important if someone is auditioning as a model but not so important for theatre. If a student is cast in a role, he or she will be asked or measured. Make sure the students always include eye and hair color. Using a generous "age range" instead of an actual age may expand the auditioners' availability. They may be fourteen but look sixteen, so get the advantage. Again, be careful that they not exaggerate.

- *Experience:* This is the most important part of the résumé. Your students should list every show, talent show, holiday production, or Grandma's family reunion in which they have participated. It doesn't matter if they were trees in the back row — list it! Of course, if they have any print or film work (TV or movies), that would be listed in its own category before Stage Experience.

- *Training:* Now's the time to brag about those piano lessons Mom made them take for six years. If they had a lesson, put it here, even if it was only a few lessons.

- *Special skills:* Anything that an auditioner can do fairly well (they don't have to be an expert) should be listed here. If they speak a language other than English, list it here as well.

Photograph

It is a great idea to include a photograph with a résumé at an audition. When there are many auditioners, the directors can often have trouble remembering from the résumé who was whom. Some auditions are taped, which helps, but the best thing actors can do to implant themselves in the director's memory is to include a photo. This can be as simple as a snapshot printed from a regular printer to a professional headshot that can be done at a local photographer or even by a friend who has a good camera. The photo should be from the shoulders up, modest, and include a wide, natural smile.

Color photos are recommended for redheads but not necessary for everyone else. An auditioner can buy glossy photo paper at a dollar store and run it through a regular printer. It can be fun to have a "photo session" with a friend or parent, experimenting with different poses, smiles, and hairstyles. They can then pick one they like and either take it to a local store and print it (printing stores even have the right paper), or print it at home. Unless someone is auditioning for a professional company, he or she does not need a professional headshot, but they're fun to do and nice to have. If one has a small snapshot (make sure it is mostly the face), just staple it to the front of the résumé. If there is a full-sized photo (8 x 10), one can paste the photo to the back of the résumé and then trim the paper so they are flush. There you go — a professional résumé and photo! This is an excellent project for the classroom, particularly if there are photography students willing to help with the photos.

Singing

Obviously, not all auditions are for musicals, but if at any time in a student's career he or she might want to audition for a musical, you could address that in class. Have your students actually research different songs — from musicals, not pop or rock music — until they find something they like and can sing in their vocal range. The next piece of this is securing the sheet music — the page from which the pianist will play at an audition. There are many online sites that offer free sheet music for almost any song. Make sure it's a full pianist copy and not from a "fake book" that only includes chords. Many pianists cannot play from that. Get a good clean copy and have them practice, practice, practice! They should be encouraged to sing in the shower and in the car. If they're afraid to sing in front of their little brother, their audition is bound to not be very powerful. If you can find a pianist (or if the school music teacher is available for a class), they should practice with someone actually playing the piano. It's a good idea to have the students audition in front of each other so they can be comfortable singing in front of people. Encourage them to sing out, smile, and not to worry about technique as much as exuding confidence.

Dancing

As with singing, this is only applicable if the student is auditioning for a musical. Dance training is always a plus, but directors and choreographers do not expect that and are pleased to have the auditioner make an effort. Even if the student has never danced before, most people are able to move comfortably and follow some simple directions. Hopefully, that's all the student will have to do. If the student is auditioning for a heavy dance show, encourage him or her to do the best he or she can. The student should wear comfortable clothes, reasonable shoes (no flip-flops or sandals *ever*), and smile. To prepare students for a dance audition, have them follow a few simple movements set to music. (Yes, you can! Think aerobics or Zumba!) It's actually really fun and good for you. Most of the time, the students really enjoy it even if they complain a little.

Auditions

There are two types of auditions with regards to reading for a role. In the first case, an actor is either given the script or piece of script, called a *side*, in advance or in the waiting room and are allowed a chance to read through it and have a good feel for what's up. A *cold reading* is being handed the reading while the auditioner is standing up at the audition. The best way to handle either of these is to be prepared and as comfortable as they can be reading in front of a group. Use the skits in this book both as cold readings (hand them the book and have them go for it), or rehearsed (memorization or group work discussing or rehearsing before performing for the class). The more they work on their posture, volume, speed of speech (most people talk far too fast), and expression, the better chance they will have at doing a good job with their reading.

Callbacks

If an actor has done a good job and the directors like him or her, he or she may be *called back* or asked to come back and try again. Congratulate the actor — it's a great step! Often, two or more people are called back for the same role so the directing staff can make their choice between their top candidates. This can be fun and a nice way to mingle with other kids, but it can also be discouraging, particularly if an actor sees someone up for the same role and feels the other actor is better. Don't allow the actor to be discouraged — you just never know what a director is looking for. It may appear that one person was wonderful but the directors cast another person, for many different reasons (size, coloring, rehearsal availability, what he or she was wearing, attitude, etc.). As with the first audition, the student should be encouraged to do the best he or she can, breathe deeply so he or she can relax, and *smile*.

1. Cross Walk

Topic: Two deer discuss the concept of crossing the highway.

Cast:
PHIL: Ambitious, excited, a real devoted guy
BUCK: A little less excited about the plan

1   PHIL: *(Determined)* I'm gonna do it.
2   BUCK: Don't do it. I'm warning you, Phil, don't do it.
3   PHIL: *(Excited)* But have you seen her? Have you seen that
4   beauty over across the highway?
5   BUCK: Yes. Have *you* seen all the cars streaming by at one
6   hundred miles per hour?
7   PHIL: So what?
8   BUCK: *(Exasperated)* So what? Didn't you hear what
9   happened to Chuck?
10   PHIL: Oh, yeah, Chuck. That was grisly.
11   BUCK: It happens every year. Some guy gets a look at some
12   girl over yonder, and *bam!*
13   PHIL: You're exaggerating. I know I can do it. I'm smart, and
14   I'm fast. Chuck was a slacker.
15   BUCK: Rest in peace.
16   PHIL: Oh, yeah, sorry Chuck, wherever you are. *(A moment*
17   *of silence.)*
18   BUCK: *(Trying to be convincing)* C'mon, Phil, forget about her.
19   It's not worth it, man.
20   PHIL: *(Excited again)* Wait, I've been watching traffic and I
21   have an idea.
22   BUCK: Great.
23   PHIL: Right around two a.m., there's almost no traffic
24   whatsoever.
25   BUCK: Almost.
26   PHIL: Right. I can make it. I'll wait for a break in traffic and

1   I'm going.

2 BUCK: All it takes is one, Phil. One big, fast car.

3 PHIL: George made out OK.

4 BUCK: You can't go by what happened to George.

5 PHIL: Oh yes I can. He ran into a car, got up, and lived to
6   play another day.

7 BUCK: George is a moron.

8 PHIL: Yes, but a *living* moron.

9 BUCK: *(Trying to be convincing)* I'm telling you, Phil, you try
10   to cross this highway and that will be the end of you.

11 PHIL: And I'm telling *you* I can make it perfectly safe.

12 BUCK: *(Sighs.)* Looks like there's no talking you out of it.

13 PHIL: It's a matter of pride, Buck. She's seen me looking at
14   her. If I don't try to go for it, she'll think I'm a wuss.

15 BUCK: A living wuss.

16 PHIL: I'm going. Tonight, two a.m.

17 BUCK: I'll tell everyone so that you can have an audience to
18   this ... event.

19 PHIL: Great, always grateful for my fans.

20 BUCK: I wish you the best of luck.

21 PHIL: I hope she likes me.

22 BUCK: She'd better after all you're going through for her.

23 PHIL: Well, I am one of a kind.

24 BUCK: You can say that again. Well, Buck, it's been great
25   knowing you.

26 PHIL: Hey, you gotta stick around. For tomorrow.

27 BUCK: What's tomorrow?

28 PHIL: I gotta figure out a way to get back.

29 BUCK: Huh?

30 PHIL: After I spend the day with her, I gotta get back home,
31   right? I gotta figure out a way to get back.

32 BUCK: *(Sighing)* This is going to be a loooong day.

2. Hang Up

Topic: A teacher and a student discuss school rules.

Cast:
MRS. Z: Just trying to do her job
MICHAEL: Just trying to be a kid

1   MRS. Z: Michael.
2   MICHAEL: Hello.
3   MRS. Z: Hi. What do you have in your pocket?
4   MICHAEL: My lunch.
5   MRS. Z: That two by three inch item in your pocket is your
6   lunch?
7   MICHAEL: *(Thoughtfully)* I'm on a diet.
8   MRS. Z: Please take out your cell phone.
9   MICHAEL: Oh, you're talking about my *phone*.
10 MRS. Z: You know you're not supposed to carry your phone
11   during class.
12 MICHAEL: I wasn't using it.
13 MRS. Z: That's not the point. You know you're not supposed
14   to carry it.
15 MICHAEL: There are so many dumb rules at this school, it's
16   hard to keep track of them all.
17 MRS. Z: Actually, Michael, every rule we have is in place for
18   a reason.
19 MICHAEL: I find that hard to believe.
20 MRS. Z: Tell me a rule and I'll tell you the reason.
21 MICHAEL: Running in the hallways.
22 MRS. Z: Two broken arms and a concussion last year alone.
23 MICHAEL: *(A little less confident)* Homework on Fridays.
24 MRS. Z: One-fifth of school takes place on Fridays. You
25   guys can't do everything we need to get done in four-
26   fifths of the time we have.

1   **MICHAEL:** *(Much less confident)* **Starting school in August.**

2   MRS. Z: Having off in December and March.

3   MICHAEL: Tests.

4   MRS. Z: Graduation.

5   MICHAEL: You have an answer for everything.

6   MRS. Z: Just trying to keep order. That's kind of how life

7   works.

8   MICHAEL: Not exactly a barrel of laughs.

9   MRS. Z: Well, I guess school isn't always designed for your

10   entertainment. Now, if I let you take your phone back to

11   your locker, will you promise to not use it on the way?

12   MICHAEL: You drive a hard bargain.

3. Halftime

Topic: The actors and the coach try to get their act together during the big game.

Cast:
COACH: Tough; trying to get the offense and defense to work
      together
MIKE: Offense
CHARLES: Offense
BRIAN: Offense
SETH: Offense
MARCUS: Offense
KEVIN: Defense
CHIP: Defense
GERRY: Defense
PALMER: Defense

1   **COACH:** *(Strong, forceful)* **Alright, men, we're going to have**
2   **to get out there and *fight* this half!** *(Everyone cheers,*
3   *agrees.)*
4   **MIKE: I'm a little confused, Coach.**
5   **COACH: About what, Mike?**
6   **MIKE: When you called forty-seven blue three red — what**
7   **did that mean?**
8   **CHARLES:** *(Sarcastically)* **It meant you were supposed to**
9   **throw the ball to me, genius.**
10 **SETH:** *(Confused)* **I thought it meant I was supposed to run**
11   **behind Chad and have the ball thrown to me.**
12 **BRIAN: I thought I was supposed to tackle the tight end so**
13   **Mike would run the ball himself.**
14 **COACH: I see where the confusion lies.**
15 **MARCUS:** *(Angry)* **The confusion lies in the defense.**
16   *(DEFENSE complains.)* **If they would maybe knock**
17   **someone down every now and then, it wouldn't be so**
18   **hard for us to score points.**

1   KEVIN: If you could catch maybe one ball a game, you could
2   score points.
3   CHIP: Yeah, Mike, our goal is *that* way. *(Pointing)*
4   COACH: *(Trying to settle them down)* OK, guys, no finger-
5   pointing. This is a *team* sport. There is no "I" in *team*.
6   MARCUS: *(Quietly)* There is in *idiot*.
7   COACH: *(Loudly)* OK, enough! Everybody has to do his part
8   to bring this team together. No one is more or less
9   important than anyone else. If the defense held a tight
10   line and kept the ball away from the other guys' goal,
11   and if the offense actually ran *toward* our goal, we would
12   definitely do better. Does that make any sense?
13   GERRY: Did you guys see Mary Jo and her new cheerleading
14   squad? Wow!
15   PALMER: Yeah, it was hard to concentrate on knocking
16   anyone down while they were doing their thing on the
17   sideline.
18   COACH: You guys have got to concentrate!
19   KEVIN: We were concentrating alright. *(High-fives guy next to*
20   *him.)*
21   COACH: Alright. *(Trying to get calm)* Alright. Here's the deal.
22   *You guys,* *(Points to the DEFENSE)* you try to knock down
23   all of their guys, especially the guy with the ball. OK?
24   *(DEFENSE mumbles assent.)* And *you guys,* *(Points to the*
25   *OFFENSE)* take the doggone ball and get it across the
26   goal line — I'll remind you which one is ours this time,
27   Mike. Just get it across the goal line any way you can.
28   Got it? *(OFFENSE mumbles assent.)*
29   GERRY: One last question, Coach?
30   COACH: What is it, Gerry?
31   GERRY: Is there pizza after the game?

4. Helping Out

Topic: Two girls try to get their friend to understand the idea of cleaning her room.

Cast:
KLOWI: Strong, devoted to getting to the mall
SARAH: Has a great lack of interest in cleaning
CASSIDY: Going along for the ride

1 **KLOWI:** *(Trying to be persuasive)* **Sarah, you have *got* to get**
2   **moving.**
3 **SARAH:** *(Whining)* **I don't feel like it.**
4 **CASSIDY:** **It doesn't matter if you feel like it, you gotta do**
5   **it.**
6 **SARAH:** *(Pouting)* **My mom is so unfair.**
7 **KLOWI:** *(Encouragingly)* **Come on, Sarah, just start.**
8 **CASSIDY:** **You wouldn't believe what I had to do before my**
9   **mom would let me leave the house.**
10 **KLOWI:** **We all have to do stuff in order to go out. Just start**
11   **picking stuff up, Sarah. Look, we'll help.**
12 **SARAH:** **It's not like the world will stop revolving if my room**
13   **isn't spotless.**
14 **CASSIDY:** **Uh, spotless?** *(Looks around.)* **Sarah, I can't even**
15   **see your floor.**
16 **KLOWI:** **What color *is* your rug?**
17 **SARAH:** **It's not that bad.**
18 **CASSIDY and KLOWI:** **Oh, yes it is.**
19 **KLOWI:** **It's actually kind of disgusting, Sarah.**
20 **SARAH:** **Like your room is perfect, Cassidy.**
21 **CASSIDY:** *(Holds up hands in protest.)* **Guilty! My room is a**
22   **mess. But *my* mother made me watch my gross little**
23   **brother for three hours this afternoon. You have it easy.**
24 **KLOWI:** **And I had to go to my mom's home decorating class**
25   **and pretend like I was fascinated. It was the most boring**

1   two hours of my life.

2 CASSIDY: Straightening up this room will take about a half

3   hour if we help. I really, really want to go to the mall.

4 SARAH: I want to go too.

5 CASSIDY: So, let's pick up the room.

6 KLOWI: *(Like it's a secret)* Here's a trick, Sarah. Don't tell

7   anyone else I told you: If you pick up everything on the

8   floor and just like throw it in drawers or closets, she'll

9   be happy. At least happy enough to let you go to the

10   mall.

11 SARAH: Well, that's not so bad.

12 CASSIDY: You'll probably have to do the rest another time,

13   but just the floor is a good start.

14 SARAH: My mom would be thrilled if she could see my floor.

15 KLOWI: Let's go then!

16 SARAH: OK. I sure hope this trip to the mall is worth it.

17 CASSIDY: It will! Jennings is having a great shoe sale.

18 KLOWI: We just have to make sure Sarah doesn't buy any

19   more shoes — there's no place in her room to store

20   them!

21 SARAH: Thanks for the help, guys.

5. Over the Limit

Topic: The wonders of the cell phone and getting in trouble because of it.

Cast:
MERCY: Dejected; very upset that she's in trouble
GARY: Trying to be a good friend
KATY: Also a good friend trying to keep Mercy out of trouble

1 MERCY: *(Dramatically)* My life is over.

2 GARY: Again?

3 KATY: What's wrong?

4 MERCY: My parents took my phone away.

5 GARY: *(Almost seriously)* How will you survive? Should I call
6   nine-one-one?

7 KATY: OK, Mercy, what did you do? It better not be gross.

8 MERCY: I went over my minutes.

9 KATY: Don't you have a monitor on your phone or
10   something to keep that from happening?

11 MERCY: I sent a couple of thousand text messages last
12   month.

13 GARY: *(Completely baffled)* How are your fingers still
14   attached to your hands?

15 KATY: Oh, Gary, knock it off. Everyone texts.

16 GARY: Not every day, all day. Some of you girls text all of
17   the time. I don't know how you have time to brush your
18   teeth.

19 MERCY: You're just not with it, Gary. It's the new form of
20   communication. Everyone does it.

21 GARY: If everyone jumped off a bridge —

22 KATY: Oh, good grief.

23 MERCY: My folks gave me a ten-hour speech about
24   "alternative forms of communication." Like my mom
25   didn't sit on the phone for the whole night when she was

1   a kid.

2 GARY: It's not the same. Talking on the phone is better than

3   texting.

4 KATY: How's that?

5 GARY: When you talk to someone, you have, like, inflection

6   and tone and stuff. It's just different.

7 MERCY: I like to talk on the phone too. I went over my

8   talking minutes too.

9 GARY: So basically you just *communicate* too much.

10 MERCY: *(Agreeing)* That's what my parents say.

11 KATY: I guess you're going to have to find something else to

12   do with your time.

13 GARY: Like homework and stuff.

14 MERCY: *(Has a good idea)* And shopping!

15 KATY: *(Excited)* And manicures!

16 MERCY: And movies! You're right, Gary, there's a lot of

17   other things I can do without my cell phone.

18 KATY: Wait, when you go to the mall, how are you gonna

19   keep me posted about the sales if you can't use your

20   phone?

21 MERCY: Oh, no! It's all falling apart again.

22 GARY: I think I'll go get a milk shake.

23 MERCY: Milk shakes! Ice cream! Let's go together and I

24   won't miss my phone.

25 GARY: Great.

6. Baby Steps

Topic: Two girls discuss adding a new member to the family.

Cast:
MISHA: Very disturbed at the "good" news
KELLY: Trying to convince Misha to see the upside

1 MISHA: I'm having an awful day.

2 KELLY: Oh no, Misha, what's wrong?

3 MISHA: *(Delivering the horrible news)* My mom's having a
4   baby.

5 KELLY: *(Surprised and excited)* Oh, that's awesome! Why are
6   you upset?

7 MISHA: You don't get it — it's going to ruin my life.

8 KELLY: How can an adorable, sweet baby ruin your life?

9 MISHA: It's going to come in and take over, that's how.

10 KELLY: Take over?

11 MISHA: *(Frustrated)* Everything will be about the baby. The
12   baby needs this, the baby needs that. Don't wake up the
13   baby. My college fund will probably go to baby food.

14 KELLY: That's silly, Misha. That's never gonna happen.

15 MISHA: My mom and dad are so excited. They can't wait.
16   It's like I don't even exist any more.

17 KELLY: Come on. Your parents are terrific. They're not like
18   that. You know they love you.

19 MISHA: I know they love me, but this is different. Babies are
20   so cute. *(A little sad)* I don't stand a chance.

21 KELLY: You're overreacting. Think about how much fun it
22   will be to have a new baby in the house.

23 MISHA: Yeah. Fun. Right.

24 KELLY: Just think about it! Baby showers, new furniture,
25   shopping for little socks!

26 MISHA: Kelly, really, socks?

1 KELLY: Yes, and tiny onesies and hats and toys! Think
2   about all the cute *Curious George* and *Madeline* books
3   you could read to him.
4 MISHA: *(Emphatic)* Her. It's gotta be a her. I couldn't stand
5   a him.
6 KELLY: OK, her. Just think, Misha, you'll be the big sister.
7 MISHA: So?
8 KELLY: So, *she'll* think you are the greatest person that ever
9   lived.
10 MISHA: *(Warming up to the idea)* Really?
11 KELLY: Really. It will always be, "Why can't you be more like
12   Misha?" and "Misha didn't get into that kind of trouble
13   when she was little."
14 MISHA: Yeah!
15 KELLY: And you can be the boss. You can tell her to do your
16   chores or threaten to not play with her or read her a
17   book.
18 MISHA: *(Coming up with her own ideas)* And, since I'm the
19   oldest, I get to set the rules like she can't come into my
20   room or get into my makeup.
21 KELLY: You don't have any makeup.
22 MISHA: I will by the time she's old enough to get into it.
23 KELLY: Now you're getting into the spirit!
24 MISHA: Yeah, I guess you're right. It will be nice to have a
25   little sister to boss around.
26 KELLY: That's not exactly what I said, but I'm glad to see
27   you're readjusting your attitude.
28 MISHA: I guess I'd better start picking out names. My
29   mother is helpless when it comes to things like that. She
30   couldn't even pick out a name for my hamster.
31 KELLY: You were more fun when you were mad.

7. Floral Expressions

Topic: A clueless guy and his friend discuss the concept of flowers and cemeteries.

Cast:
ELI: Confident; excited about the great thing he's done
PIERRE: Trying to knock some sense into Eli

1 **ELI:** *(Confident and content)* **I'm all set for a year's worth of**
2 **brownie points.**
3 **PIERRE: How's that?**
4 **ELI: I got a huge bunch of flowers for my mom.**
5 **PIERRE: For what?**
6 **ELI: Just because. You're supposed to give your mom**
7 **flowers and stuff.**
8 **PIERRE: Since when?**
9 **ELI: Since always. You're just not hip like me.**
10 **PIERRE: OK, what have you done wrong so you have to give**
11 **your mother flowers?**
12 **ELI: Me? Absolutely nothing.** *(Smiles.)*
13 **PIERRE: Yeah like I believe that.**
14 **ELI: Trust me, it has absolutely nothing to do with either my**
15 **grades or certain vases in the house that I may or may**
16 **not have broken.**
17 **PIERRE: So you broke a vase and you're flunking science**
18 **and you decided to get your mother flowers.**
19 **ELI: That's about the size of it.**
20 **PIERRE: I guess it makes sense in a perverted Eli-type of way.**
21 **ELI:** *(Not very sincerely)* **Gee thanks.**
22 **PIERRE: Mind me asking where you got money for flowers?**
23 **ELI: No money required. You know I never have any money.**
24 **They were free.**
25 **PIERRE:** *(Sensing disaster)* **Free?**
26 **ELI: Just sitting there, free for the taking.**

1   PIERRE: I know I'm going to regret asking this, but I will
2   anyway: Just sitting where?
3   ELI: I was walking down Albany Court and saw a field with
4   lots of flowers, all sorts of flowers, just lying there.
5   PIERRE: Albany Court? Off Roadway Street?
6   ELI: Yep, that's the place.
7   PIERRE: Eli, that's a cemetery.
8   ELI: No it's not.
9   PIERRE: It's a pet cemetery. I swear.
10 ELI: *(Completely shocked)* A what?
11 PIERRE: A pet cemetery. Some people take their dead pets to
12   the cemetery — you know, a graveyard? And I guess some
13   people put flowers on the graves. You just stole some poor
14   sad person's flowers they left for their dead pet.
15 ELI: Not possible. Although I was curious why a perfectly
16   good bunch of flowers were just lying there on the
17   ground, all wrapped up nicely.
18 PIERRE: You have to put them back.
19 ELI: I can't! I already gave them to my mother.
20 PIERRE: Well, you'll have to replace them then. Go to the
21   store and buy another bunch. It's the right thing to do
22   and you know it.
23 ELI: I have absolutely no money.
24 PIERRE: You know Mr. Lewenstein will pay you to mow his
25   lawn. Go do it now.
26 ELI: *(Sighs.)* Here I was trying to do something nice and it
27   backfires on me.
28 PIERRE: Mowing an old man's lawn for like twenty bucks is
29   not the end of the world. It will do you good to earn
30   money for a change. And you'll probably have money
31   leftover and can buy me a burger.
32 ELI: Maybe you should go mow someone's lawn and buy *me*
33   a burger.
34 PIERRE: Maybe we should both earn our own money and buy
35   some *girls* burgers.
36 ELI: I like where this is going!

8. Valentines

Topic: Two girls discuss the most romantic day of the year.

Cast:
MELI: Optimistic; looking forward to the big day
PENNY: A little disillusioned about guys' abilities to be romantic

1   MELI: *(Very happy and excited)* **I'm so excited about Friday.**
2   PENNY: **What's Friday?**
3   MELI: **You're kidding right?**
4   PENNY: **No, really, is something going on I don't know**
5   **about?**
6   MELI: **It's Valentine's Day!**
7   PENNY: **Oh, right.** *(Blandly)* **Big deal.**
8   MELI: **Big deal? Are you kidding? It's only the most**
9   **important day of the year.**
10 PENNY: **Most important day of the year? In what world?**
11 MELI: **Oh, come on, Penny. You're not excited about all the**
12   **possibilities?**
13 PENNY: **Which possibilities would they be?**
14 MELI: **All the boys who are going to bring me cards and**
15   **presents.**
16 PENNY: *(As if she feels sorry for her)* **Oh, Meli, really? You**
17   **really think that?**
18 MELI: **Of course! I know Brandon has a thing for me, and**
19   **Casey's been smiling at me a lot. Who knows how many**
20   **boys are out there just waiting for the opportunity to**
21   **show me their affections?**
22 PENNY: **Let me tell you how this is going to work, Meli.**
23   **You'll come to school all dressed up and excited and**
24   **then every boy in school is going to completely ignore**
25   **you.**
26 MELI: *(Confident)* **Never gonna happen.**

1 PENNY: Is certainly going to happen. You just don't know
2   anything about men.
3 MELI: And you do?
4 PENNY: I know enough to know that no middle school boy
5   is going to embarrass himself by bringing stuff for a girl
6   on Valentine's Day. I don't know one guy at school who
7   has the guts to do that.
8 MELI: You're wrong. Brandon and Casey will be at my feet. I
9   think Chris likes me too. Oh, who am I going to choose?
10 PENNY: You're so deluded.
11 MELI: Why do you think boys won't recognize Valentine's
12   Day, the most important, romantic day of the year?
13 PENNY: That's the very reason. Valentine's Day is created
14   by women, I'm convinced of it. It's a day to force men to
15   publicly proclaim their love for a girl. No guy wants to do
16   that. Trust me, you're better off not expecting anything.
17   That way, you won't be disappointed.
18 MELI: Well, I hate to think that's true, but I can see where
19   they might be uncomfortable expressing themselves so
20   publicly. Maybe I'll just get anonymous cards in my
21   locker.
22 PENNY: You might get a FacePage notice. That's about the
23   extent of these guys' creativity.
24 MELI: FacePage? That's it?
25 PENNY: Take what you can get. Myself, I don't expect
26   anyone to even acknowledge the day. I know I won't.
27 MELI: You don't have a romantic bone in your body.
28 PENNY: No I don't. And I'm perfectly happy just the way I
29   am.
30 MELI: And you don't plan on sending cards or notes to *any*
31   guy?
32 PENNY: Absolutely not. I'm not ready to face the
33   embarrassment either. And don't *you* go getting any
34   ideas about giving cards or anything to anyone. You'll
35   just humiliate yourself.

1 MELI: If you say so. *(Dreamy)* I still think it would be
2   romantic if someone gave me flowers, or a present, or
3   cards.
4 PENNY: Maybe someday. Not in middle school.
5 MELI: *(Sighs.)* I can't wait til high school. Boys are so much
6   more mature in high school.
7 PENNY: You sure have a lot to learn.

9. Clean Up

Topic: Trying to rally kids to work on cleaning up the local park.

Cast:
AURORA: The leader; trying to motivate the other kids
KEIRA: Excited, energetic, enthusiastic
EMMETT: Only here for the food
BLAKE: Not 100% onboard but willing to consider the opportunity

1 AURORA: **Come on, guys, let's get this meeting going.**

2 KEIRA: *(Lots of energy)* **I'm so excited. We are going to make**
3   **such an impact on the community.**

4 EMMETT: **Will there be food? I'm not working unless they**
5   **feed me.**

6 HANNAH: **Emmett, why are you even here?**

7 BLAKE: **He's here for the food, didn't you hear?**

8 KEIRA: *(All business)* **This is not about food. We're talking**
9   **about cleaning up Deer Park on Saturday the sixteenth.**
10   **Didn't you know that when you signed up?**

11 EMMETT: **I'm all for helping clean up the park. I'm just**
12   **saying I was hoping to be fed once I get there.**

13 AURORA: **We need to put together some posters and get**
14   **more help. Who wants to be in charge of posters?**

15 HANNAH: **I nominate Blake.**

16 BLAKE: *(Not thrilled to be nominated)* **Me? Why?**

17 HANNAH: **You're the best artist in the group.**

18 EMMETT: **He's also the laziest. Don't ask him to do**
19   **anything.**

20 KEIRA: **Everybody has to pitch in to make this committee**
21   **work. I think we should work on the posters together.**
22   **Everybody tell their parents they're staying after school**
23   **on Thursday to work on the committee.**

24 BLAKE: **Thursday is baseball.**

25 HANNAH: **Ballet.**

1 EMMETT: Half-price pizza at Nick's Pizza Palace.
2 KEIRA: Come on, guys, we have to find a day when we can
3   meet. What days are you free?
4 BLAKE: Friday.
5 HANNAH: I can do Friday.
6 EMMETT: No good deals on food on Friday. That will work.
7 AURORA: *(Happy to get on with things)* OK, we'll meet
8   Friday. I'll even bring a bag of chips.
9 EMMETT: I'm there!
10 AURORA: OK, we're gonna make posters. What else do we
11   need to get?
12 KEIRA: Well, we need trash bags, and gloves I guess.
13 HANNAH: Definitely gloves. I don't want to touch any of
14   that gross stuff at Deer Park.
15 AURORA: So where can we get this stuff?
16 BLAKE: My uncle works at Dane's Hardware. Maybe he can
17   get it for us for free.
18 AURORA: That would be great!
19 EMMETT: *(A little more enthusiastically)* Maybe we could
20   make an announcement one morning to get more
21   helpers.
22 HANNAH: I nominate Emmett to make the announcement.
23 EMMETT: Why me?
24 HANNAH: Because you have the best speaking voice.
25 EMMETT: *(Very dramatically)* Why, thank you very much.
26 KEIRA: I still think we need some adults to help. Can we get
27   Mrs. Carter to put something in the weekly school
28   newsletter asking for help?
29 AURORA: That's a great idea! Since we're now officially the
30   Environmental Club, we can put an announcement in the
31   newsletter.
32 BLAKE: We're officially the Environmental Club?
33 EMMETT: Yeah, Blake, you must have slept through that
34   part of the meeting.
35 AURORA: I think if we have like ten more people, we should

1   be able to make a huge dent in the trash along the fence.

2   That's where I want to focus.

3 HANNAH: Maybe we could put up posters by the park, too,

4   like a couple of days before telling the neighborhood

5   what we're doing. Maybe people will come by to help.

6 EMMETT: If nothing else, maybe someone will bring a box of

7   donuts.

8 KEIRA: Will you forget about the donuts? Jeez! Eat before

9   you come.

10. Airborne

Topic: Two flies find themselves aboard an airplane.

Cast:

LAM: Confused and worried
NAL: A little more confident but still in the wrong place at the wrong
    time

1   LAM: *(Dazed)* **Where are we? What's going on?**

2   NAL: **I think we got on an airplane.**

3   LAM: *(Confused)* **A what?**

4   NAL: **I knew this was going to happen. I should never have**

5   **followed that guy's soda in here.**

6   LAM: **What are you talking about?**

7   NAL: **And** *you* **should know better than to follow me. You**

8   **know I never watch where I'm flying.**

9   LAM: **I don't understand. I'm so confused ... So** *where* **are**

10   **we?**

11 NAL: **It's called an airplane. It's a form of transportation. It**

12   **takes the people from one place to another.**

13 LAM: **Like a car?**

14 NAL: **Sort of. But not really. It goes a bit further than a car.**

15 LAM: **Like how much further?**

16 NAL: **Like Detroit. Or Mexico. I have no idea. I didn't look**

17   **at the signs.**

18 LAM: *(Starting to get worried and frightened)* **So you have no**

19   **idea where we're going? What are we going to do?**

20 NAL: **You're asking me? I'm the one that followed that guy's**

21   **soda into an enclosed place. And I didn't even get any.**

22 LAM: **Well, is there any food? What are we supposed to eat?**

23   **How long will we be in here?**

24 NAL: **I have no idea. Could be an hour or two, could be a**

25   **day or two.**

26 LAM: **Wait a minute — isn't our lifespan kind of short?**

1 NAL: I don't want to think about that. Let's look for food.
2 LAM: Those people up there have everything covered and
3   they don't look like they're in any hurry to uncover stuff.
4 NAL: OK, let's fly around and see what we can find.
5 LAM: If I don't see you again, it was nice knowing you.
6 NAL: Well, at least we're having an adventure. Beats the
7   dump any day.
8 LAM: Meet you back here in an hour. If you find anything to
9   eat, bring some for me.
10 NAL: Will do.

11. Musical Lessons

Topic: The pros and cons of taking piano lessons.

Cast:
GABBY: Not exactly into the idea of the lessons
LEANA: Trying to be encouraging; a real music lover

1   GABBY: *(Whining)* I really, really don't want to go.
2   LEANA: Go where?
3   GABBY: Piano lessons. I have to go after school today.
4   LEANA: I thought you liked playing piano.
5   GABBY: I do. I just hate lessons.
6   LEANA: Why?
7   GABBY: My teacher's mean. She always yells at me for not
8   practicing.
9   LEANA: Why don't you practice then?
10 GABBY: Thanks a lot. You sound like my mother.
11 LEANA: If you hate it so much, why do you keep going?
12 GABBY: My mom makes me. She says I'll be sorry if I stop.
13 LEANA: You probably will. I know a zillion kids who took
14   lessons for like a year and then quit. Now they're all
15   sorry they can't play anything.
16 GABBY: I know. I really like playing. I can play some cool
17   songs, too.
18 LEANA: I know. You played "Happy Birthday" at Meghan's
19   party and it was cool. Everyone was impressed.
20 GABBY: Well, I can play more than "Happy Birthday." I'm
21   learning Bach and Chopin and Mozart.
22 LEANA: *(Impressed)* That's really cool. I think you should
23   keep taking lessons.
24 GABBY: What about my mean teacher?
25 LEANA: Seems like you have two choices. A, you could
26   actually practice like you're supposed to. B, you could

1   ask your mom if you could find a different teacher.

2   GABBY: *(Thoughtfully)* I never thought of that.

3   LEANA: Music Palace gives lessons. I hear there's a guy

4   there who teaches and is good. He's cute too.

5   GABBY: *(Excited)* Really? A cute piano teacher? That would

6   be awesome.

7   LEANA: I knew that would get your attention. You know,

8   you're still going to have to practice, at least

9   occasionally.

10 GABBY: Yeah, but if I had a teacher who didn't yell at me all

11   the time, maybe I'd want to practice.

12 LEANA: If you practiced maybe the teacher wouldn't yell.

13 GABBY: You're really a lot of help.

14 LEANA: Always glad to be of assistance.

12. Pasta People Pleaser

Topic: A boss and his employee discuss the employee's business report.

Cast:
MR. LANDON: Just trying to keep the office running smoothly
JOHNSON: A little clueless, but lots of energy

1   *(MR. LANDON is sitting at a desk.)*
2 **JOHNSON:** *(Coming in the room)* **You sent for me, boss?**
3 **MR. LANDON:** *(Beckoning)* **Yes, Johnson, come in. Have a**
4   **seat.** *(JOHNSON sits.)*
5 **JOHNSON: I see you have my business report there.**
6 **MR. LANDON:** *(Hesitantly)* **Yes, well, that's what I wanted to**
7   **talk about.**
8 **JOHNSON: I worked very hard on that.**
9 **MR. LANDON: Yes, I can see that. I see this first page is the**
10   **customer chart — very nice.**
11 **JOHNSON:** *(Pleased)* **Thanks.**
12 **MR. LANDON:** *(Hesitantly)* **It's this second page I'm**
13   **concerned about.**
14 **JOHNSON: Really?**
15 **MR. LANDON: Yeah. It's a recipe for spaghetti sauce.**
16 **JOHNSON: Grandma's award-winning marinara sauce, to**
17   **be exact.** *(Points to the page.)* **See, there's the title right**
18   **there.**
19 **MR. LANDON: Right, my mistake.** *(Rolls eyes.)* **Can you**
20   **explain why there's a recipe in the middle of your**
21   **business report?**
22 **JOHNSON: Well, I would think that would be perfectly**
23   **obvious.**
24 **MR. LANDON: Actually, it's not obvious in any way.**
25 **JOHNSON: You wanted my findings on customer**
26   **satisfaction, right?**

1 MR. LANDON: Right.
2 JOHNSON: Well, there you have it. Guaranteed to give you
3   customer satisfaction.
4 MR. LANDON: I still don't get it.
5 JOHNSON: See, I think we should have a pasta dinner to
6   thank all of our customers for their business.
7 MR. LANDON: You do?
8 JOHNSON: Sure, we could use the local fire hall. A big
9   pasta dinner.
10 MR. LANDON: The fire hall.
11 JOHNSON: Absolutely. We can send out a nice invitation to
12   every customer we've had this year. We'll have all the
13   employees wait on the customers. Maybe a band.
14 MR. LANDON: I'm beginning to understand.
15 JOHNSON: Don't you think that would be a great event?
16 MR. LANDON: A spaghetti dinner.
17 JOHNSON: Grandma's award-winning marinara sauce
18   pasta dinner.
19 MR. LANDON: OK, Johnson, I think I have all the
20   information I need.
21 JOHNSON: You really love the report, huh?
22 MR. LANDON: *(As sincerely as he can possibly sound)* I can't
23   begin to tell you how I feel about this report.
24 JOHNSON: Well *(Slyly)* if that means that raise I've been
25   trying to get, I'm all for it.
26 MR. LANDON: I think you'll be hearing from the front office
27   real soon.
28 JOHNSON: *(Excitedly)* Really? That's great!
29 MR. LANDON: You'd better get back to work, I guess.
30 JOHNSON: Thanks, Mr. Landon. Oh, boy, Grandma will be
31   so excited. *(Exits.)*
32 MR. LANDON: Being the boss can be so much fun. *(Drops*
33   *head to his hands.)*

13. Rainy Day

Topic: Three kids try to figure out what to do on a long, boring day.

Cast:

JINX: Unhappy about being stuck in the house on a rainy day
CLAUDIA: Also bored, but gets excited about the new idea
MARIA: A little boy crazy; happy to find something to do

1   **JINX:** *(Lying on the floor)* **I'm so bored.**
2   **CLAUDIA:** *(Sitting on a chair, doing her nails)* **We gotta find**
3   **something to do.**
4   **MARIA: Wanna play video games?**
5   **KATY: We've been doing that for like four hours.**
6   **JINX:** *(Really whiny)* **I'm boooored.**
7   **MARIA:** *(With irritation)* **You said that already.**
8   **CLAUDIA: It feels like it's been raining for a week.**
9   **KATY: The weatherman says we're in a low pressure.**
10   **JINX: Is that supposed to mean something?**
11   **MARIA: Wanna play a board game?**
12   **JINX:** *(Blandly)* **You gotta be kidding.**
13   **CLAUDIA: Hey, Maria, maybe your mom would take us to**
14   **the mall.**
15   **MARIA: No, she won't. She already said.**
16   **KATY: If we don't find something to do soon, I'm gonna go**
17   **crazy.**
18   **JINX:** *(Sudden inspiration)* **Hey, why don't we call someone?**
19   **MARIA: Like, just call someone?**
20   **JINX: Yeah, we could like call Brittany Winston and tell her**
21   **she's the best-looking girl in school.**
22   **CLAUDIA: Yeah, we'll watch while you make that call.**
23   **JINX: I didn't mean *me*. I want *you* to call her.**
24   **KATY: Not gonna happen, Jinx.**
25   **MARIA: Why don't we call Michael Jennings?**
26   **CLAUDIA:** *(Devilish)* **Ooooh, that's a good idea.**

1 KATY: Yeah, Jinx, call Michael Jennings.

2 JINX: Why would I want to do that?

3 CLAUDIA: Ask him if he's going to the dance.

4 JINX: You want me to call Michael and ask him if he's going
5   to the dance.

6 KATY: Yes! Every girl in school is waiting for him to decide
7   who he's taking.

8 JINX: So one of you call him.

9 CLAUDIA: We can't do that.

10 MARIA: Gosh, Jinx, think about it: If we call, he'll know we
11   like him.

12 JINX: And if I call him — he'll think I'm weird.

13 CLAUDIA: Everyone already knows you're weird.

14 KATY: You owe us.

15 JINX: I have a better idea: Why don't we watch a movie?

16 MARIA: A movie?

17 CLAUDIA: There is that new Johnny Winston movie I've
18   been dying to see.

19 KATY: Right! I think we could walk up to the Movie Box and
20   rent it — it was available yesterday.

21 MARIA: I think Jinx should walk up to Movie Box, since he's
22   so unwilling to do us the one tiny favor we asked.

23 JINX: In the rain?

24 MARIA: I have an umbrella.

25 JINX: Whoever said girls made good friends was crazy.

14. Lunch Break

Topic: Two guys discuss the new menu in the cafeteria.

Cast:
JACK: The bearer of sad news
J.R.: Appalled by the changes at school

1   JACK: What did you bring for lunch today?

2   J.R.: I didn't. I'm gonna buy lunch.

3   JACK: You're gonna buy lunch ... from the cafeteria?

4   J.R.: Yeah, what of it?

5   JACK: Well, it was nice knowing you, J.R.

6   J.R.: What do you mean by that?

7   JACK: When was the last time you ate at the cafeteria?

8   J.R.: I don't know — a couple of weeks ago.

9   JACK: What did you have?

10 J.R.: I don't remember ... pizza?

11 JACK: Gone.

12 J.R.: What do you mean, "gone"?

13 JACK: They don't sell pizza anymore.

14 J.R.: They don't sell pizza anymore? In the cafeteria?

15 JACK: Oh, you haven't been following the announcements,
16   have you?

17 J.R.: No, I never listen to announcements. What are you
18   talking about?

19 JACK: The cafeteria has gone ... healthy.

20 J.R.: Healthy? What does that mean?

21 JACK: It means salad, yogurt, and tofu. That's what it
22   means.

23 J.R.: You've got to be kidding.

24 JACK: Milk instead of soda, whole wheat pasta instead of
25   regular spaghetti ...

26 J.R.: I don't think I'm hungry anymore.

1   JACK: They're trying to teach us the "nutritional value" of
2   certain fiber-rich foods.
3   J.R.: You sound like an announcement — one that I would
4   normally not listen to.
5   JACK: Lots of fresh fruit, veggies — vitamin-rich foods.
6   J.R.: How long has this been going on?
7   JACK: About two weeks. You must have had the last piece
8   of pizza in the school.
9   J.R.: If only I'd known, I would have stocked up and stored
10   some extra in my locker.
11   JACK: Now if you want junk food, you have to bring it from
12   home.
13   J.R.: What do you have for lunch?
14   JACK: I think I've got tuna with fat-free mayo, chopped
15   carrots, and yogurt.
16   J.R.: What? Jack, have you gone to the dark side too?
17   JACK: My mom thought the whole nutrition thing was such
18   a good idea, she's starting to cook like that too.
19   J.R.: And you're still living to tell the tale?
20   JACK: It's actually not too bad. She puts a little dill in the
21   tuna fish.
22   J.R.: You're starting to scare me.
23   JACK: It's good. You know, it wouldn't hurt you to eat a little
24   better.
25   J.R.: Are you suggesting that the average teenager junk-
26   food diet is no good?
27   JACK: I'm saying it wouldn't hurt all of us to eat a little less
28   junk, that's all.
29   J.R.: Maybe. No Brussels sprouts, no matter what you say.
30   JACK: No nutritional campaign in the world would get me to
31   eat Brussels sprouts.
32   J.R.: At least we can agree on that.

15. Cat Nap

Topic: Two cats try to make their peace living in the same house.

Cast:
PATCHES: Arrogant, defensive; thinks he's the boss
JERRY: Nice guy; just trying to get along

1   PATCHES: *(Suspiciously)* **What are you doing here?**
2   JERRY: What do you mean, what am I doing here? I live
3   here.
4   PATCHES: I mean in this room, at this moment. Near me.
5   You know the rules.
6   JERRY: I can go anywhere I want. I was here first.
7   PATCHES: But they like me better. You scratch the
8   furniture.
9   JERRY: I can't help it! My nails itch.
10   PATCHES: Right.
11   JERRY: Besides, you're the one who cries all night and
12   wakes everybody up.
13   PATCHES: *(Defensively)* I do not.
14   JERRY: Look, it looks like we're gonna be stuck in the same
15   household for a long time. We may as well be at least
16   civil to each other.
17   PATCHES: Never.
18   JERRY: And we have to share a food and water bowl. We
19   might as well be related.
20   PATCHES: Listen, you scurvy cat. I was living here, happy as
21   a clam and totally at peace until they heard your pathetic
22   story and decided you needed to come live here, too.
23   JERRY: It was not pathetic. I had a very traumatic
24   experience.
25   PATCHES: Whatever. The point is, I was head cat until you
26   butted in. So I get to make the rules.

1   JERRY: Oh you do, do you?

2   PATCHES: Yes. I get food and water first. I get this spot in
3   the window for the majority of the day. And when I want
4   to sit with the boss, you keep clear. Understand?

5   JERRY: You're pretty full of yourself, aren't you?

6   PATCHES: I know that I'm marvelous, if that's what you
7   mean.

8   JERRY: Well, I think you're just gonna have to get used to
9   the idea that things are gonna change around here now
10   that I've come.

11 PATCHES: I don't like that one bit.

12 JERRY: Yes, I know. But tough. You probably came here as
13   a kitten, right?

14 PATCHES: Right.

15 JERRY: Well, I lived somewhere else and it wasn't good.
16   They didn't take care of me — sometimes I didn't have
17   food for three days.

18 PATCHES: Three days?

19 JERRY: I never once got to sit with my old boss. They didn't
20   really want or like me. I don't know why I ever went there
21   in the first place. But then your boss brought me here
22   and, despite *you* being here, this is a great place to live.

23 PATCHES: It is pretty fabulous.

24 JERRY: All I can eat.

25 PATCHES: All the sunshine you could want.

26 JERRY: Lots of lap time.

27 PATCHES: No little kids chasing me.

28 JERRY: So, you see, it's only fair that you share the wealth.

29 PATCHES: *(Considering)* Hmmmm ... I guess there *is* room for
30   you to live here, too, as long as you stay out of the way.

31 JERRY: I'm sure we can work out some sort of arrangement.

32 PATCHES: I get this window, or no deal.

33 JERRY: You can have the window.

34 PATCHES: Alright. And I get the food first.

35 JERRY: Obviously.

16. Compu-Speak

Topic: The Internet can be a dangerous place.

Cast:
CHRIS: Guy/girl who has been surfing in some of the wrong places
PAT: Guy/girl, friend to Chris, trying to bring some logic to the
situation

1 **CHRIS:** *(Sad and low)* **I'm totally busted.**
2 **PAT: What happened?**
3 **CHRIS: My parents saw some chat stuff I had and**
4 **completely took away my Internet privileges.**
5 **PAT: What do you mean they saw it?**
6 **CHRIS: My mom has some sort of monitoring software on**
7 **the computer.**
8 **PAT: They did that and didn't tell you?**
9 **CHRIS: No, they told me. I knew about it.**
10 **PAT: Well why were you messing around on the web if you**
11 **knew they could find out?**
12 **CHRIS: I never thought they would actually check.**
13 **PAT: What were you doing?**
14 **CHRIS: Absolutely nothing. I was just chatting.**
15 **PAT: With who?**
16 **CHRIS: Some guy.**
17 **PAT: What guy?**
18 **CHRIS: I don't know, just some guy I met on the Internet.**
19 **PAT: You were chatting with a stranger?**
20 **CHRIS: It's no big deal.**
21 **PAT: What do you mean no big deal? They talk about it**
22 **nonstop at school.**
23 **CHRIS: It was nothing.**
24 **PAT: You don't know that. If you didn't know this guy, he**
25 **could have been anybody. He could have been like**
26 **stalking you.**

1   CHRIS: Oh, good grief. It was nothing like that. We were
2   talking about soccer, that's all.
3   PAT: You didn't tell him where you played, did you?
4   CHRIS: No, we never got that far.
5   PAT: Wow, Chris, you're crazy. Don't you know how much
6   trouble you could have gotten into?
7   CHRIS: I'm *in* trouble. I told you I was grounded.
8   PAT: I don't mean with your parents, I meant with him. He
9   could have been dangerous.
10 CHRIS: Nah.
11 PAT: You don't know! You don't know what kind of people
12   are out there. Didn't they tell you all this in computer
13   class?
14 CHRIS: I never thought anything bad would happen to me.
15 PAT: Well, you're lucky it didn't. Maybe this was a good
16   thing in disguise.
17 CHRIS: How could that possibly be? My mom said no
18   Internet for like a month!
19 PAT: Maybe you'll learn to stop talking to strangers online.
20   Don't you have enough friends you can talk with?
21 CHRIS: I just did it for fun.
22 PAT: It wouldn't have been so fun if he had turned out to be
23   a stalker.
24 CHRIS: I guess you're right.
25 PAT: If you ever get your Internet privileges back, you can
26   chat with me, anytime.
27 CHRIS: You are kind of boring, but I guess you're better than
28   nothing.
29 PAT: Thanks a lot!

17. Pep Talk

Topic: The coach and a student athlete discuss the importance of keeping grades up.

Cast:
JEREMY: Boy who just wants to play ball and not too concerned about school work
COACH: Nice guy; trying to help one of his players

1 JEREMY: *(Entering)* **You wanted to see me, Coach?**
2 COACH: *(Sitting at a desk, gestures.)* **Yeah, Jeremy, hi. Have**
3   **a seat.**
4 JEREMY: **What's up?**
5 COACH: **Principal Gomez sent me a copy of your grades.**
6 JEREMY: **Uh-oh.**
7 COACH: **Yeah. It's not pretty, let me tell you.**
8 JEREMY: **I can actually explain almost all of it.**
9 COACH: **Go ahead, give it a try.**
10 JEREMY: **Well, Mrs. Presley hates me, Tommy Simpkins**
11   **sits behind me during history and talks the whole time,**
12   **my dog ate my science homework, and Spanish — well,**
13   **I just stink at Spanish.**
14 COACH: **Those are pretty lame excuses, Jeremy.**
15 JEREMY: **Yeah, that was the best I could do on short notice.**
16 COACH: **The bottom line is you have to bring your grades up**
17   **or you can't play ball.**
18 JEREMY: *(Shocked)* **What?**
19 COACH: **Academics are the most important thing here at**
20   **the Horton School. We can't have kids playing sports**
21   **who can't keep their grades up.**
22 JEREMY: **But I hate school.**
23 COACH: **Then you can't play.**
24 JEREMY: **Basketball is all I have to live for.**
25 COACH: **Well, that's kind of dramatic, but it's the rules.**

1   JEREMY: What am I supposed to do?

2   COACH: Well, let's start with Mrs. Presley.

3   JEREMY: Oh, her.

4   COACH: I happen to know she's an excellent English teacher

5   and all the other kids seem to get along with her quite

6   well.

7   JEREMY: I'm telling you, she hates me.

8   COACH: You need to go up to her after class or after school

9   and tell her you need help.

10 JEREMY: Ouch.

11 COACH: You can do it, Jeremy. You gotta do this if you want

12   to play. And you know the big tournament is coming up.

13 JEREMY: *(Frustrated)* I know, I know. What else?

14 COACH: Tell Tommy Simpkins to stop talking.

15 JEREMY: I don't think he'll listen. He's twice as big as me.

16 COACH: Ask him nicely. And about the science homework

17   — you don't have a dog.

18 JEREMY: Yeah, I knew that was a bad excuse when I said it.

19 COACH: Which means you're just not trying. And Spanish,

20   too. Come on, Jeremy, you have to just buckle down and

21   start putting your mind to it. I know you can do it.

22 JEREMY: If you say so.

23 COACH: I say so. You can even bring your homework down

24   here during lunchtime if you want some help, or just

25   some company.

26 JEREMY: Thanks, Coach. That's great.

27 COACH: Not sure how much help I'll be in Spanish, though.

28 JEREMY: Trust me, nothing will help me in Spanish.

29 COACH: Maybe we should talk to Senorita Walsh.

30 JEREMY: Now you're just being mean.

18. Drivers Ed

Topic: An instructor and a student have an interesting driving lesson.

Cast:
INSTRUCTOR: Calm, kind; just trying to do his job
FARRIS: Quite possibly the worst driver in all of history; clueless

1   *(Both actors sitting side by side, as if in a car)*
2   INSTRUCTOR: So, Farris, are you ready to put the car in
3   reverse?
4   FARRIS: Which button is that?
5   INSTRUCTOR: It's not a button, it's the gear shift.
6   FARRIS: Huh?
7   INSTRUCTOR: *(Points.)* This shift right here. See where the
8   indicator says "D, D2, R, and P"?
9   FARRIS: Sounds like the grades on my last report card.
10   INSTRUCTOR: Right. Anyway, right now we're in "P" for
11   "Park."
12   FARRIS: Makes perfect sense.
13   INSTRUCTOR: Since we want to back out of this space,
14   which gear do you think you want to shift into?
15   FARRIS: *(Looks around.)* I don't see a "B."
16   INSTRUCTOR: "B"?
17   FARRIS: "B" for "Back out." Yeah, none of those on my
18   report card.
19   INSTRUCTOR: No, Farris, it's "R" for "Reverse."
20   FARRIS: Ooooh, that makes perfect sense.
21   INSTRUCTOR: OK, so you want to put the gear in reverse
22   — *(Throws hands forward) wait!* Sorry, didn't mean to
23   shout. I just want to make sure you prepare before you
24   move the car.
25   FARRIS: Sure, no problem. I scare myself sometimes.
26   INSTRUCTOR: *(Trying to calm himself)* OK, so, before we put

41

1   the car in reverse, what do you need to do?
2 FARRIS: Pray?
3 INSTRUCTOR: After that.
4 FARRIS: Not a clue.
5 INSTRUCTOR: You need to check the rearview mirror.
6 FARRIS: Why?
7 INSTRUCTOR: Well ... to make sure there are no
8   pedestrians or other cars behind us.
9 FARRIS: Oh, yeah, that would be bad.
10 INSTRUCTOR: So, you're buckled in. You've stored your cell
11   phone far, far away —
12 FARRIS: Wait a minute — what?
13 INSTRUCTOR: You need to put your cell phone away before
14   you start driving.
15 FARRIS: What's up with that?
16 INSTRUCTOR: It's against the law — not to mention
17   extremely unsafe — to text or talk on your phone while
18   driving.
19 FARRIS: How about eating? I was hoping to pull through
20   Pete's for a burger.
21 INSTRUCTOR: Farris, I would strongly advise you against
22   any deliberate distractions of any sort.
23 FARRIS: So that's a no?
24 INSTRUCTOR: That's a no.
25 FARRIS: So what am I supposed to be doing while I'm
26   driving?
27 INSTRUCTOR: *(Pause)* I'll tell you what, Farris. Why don't we
28   get out of the car.
29 FARRIS: What? Why?
30 INSTRUCTOR: My life insurance policy hasn't gone into
31   effect yet.
32 FARRIS: Say what?
33 INSTRUCTOR: They don't pay me enough to teach you to
34   drive. Out of the car.

19. Homework

Topic: Two students discuss the benefits of actually doing homework.

Cast:
DANI: Guy/girl who studies hard; trying to succeed
MEL: Guy/girl who is a bit of a slacker; not too concerned about school

1 DANI: I have so much homework tonight.
2 MEL: I don't have any.
3 DANI: How is that possible? You're in the same classes as I
4 am.
5 MEL: I finished it all in school.
6 DANI: Do your parents really believe that?
7 MEL: Yes.
8 DANI: You're crazy. Report cards are coming out in like two
9 weeks and your grades are gonna be terrible.
10 MEL: I don't care about that.
11 DANI: You're gonna care! Don't you remember last spring
12 when you were grounded forever because your grades
13 were so bad?
14 MEL: Yeah. I forgot about that.
15 DANI: How could you forget about it? I remember and it
16 wasn't even me.
17 MEL: I just hate homework so much. And "Bride and
18 Groom" is on tonight.
19 DANI: If you did your homework right after school, you'd be
20 done in time to see "Bride and Groom."
21 MEL: But I don't want to.
22 DANI: Nobody wants to. You think I go home from school
23 every day thinking, "I can't wait to catch up on my
24 algebra!"
25 MEL: No, Dani, I don't think you're crazy.

1 DANI: But last year when I got good grades my parents
2   extended my curfew *and* got me unlimited texting on my
3   phone.
4 MEL: No way!
5 DANI: Parents are really into the "showing responsibility"
6   thing.
7 MEL: Yeah, I guess. I hear a lot of "not showing potential"
8   and "missing opportunities," that sort of thing.
9 DANI: It must be a pain to have to hear all that.
10 MEL: I hate it.
11 DANI: Enough to do geometry?
12 MEL: I didn't say that.
13 DANI: Think about it, Mel. If you did your homework and got
14   decent grades, maybe your parents would even let you
15   go to the dance in May.
16 MEL: No ... do you think so?
17 DANI: *(Smiling)* It's nice to have a dream.
18 MEL: Will you go through your planner and show me what
19   homework we have?
20 DANI: You don't even bother to write it down anymore?
21 MEL: Not really. I know yours is more complete than mine.
22 DANI: I'll help you today, but you're on your own from now
23   on.
24 MEL: You drive a hard bargain.

20. Baby Talk

Topic: Two babies discuss the trials and tribulations of life as a baby.

Cast:
DARLING: Guy/girl; typical baby
SWEETIE: Guy/girl; typical baby

1   *(Do not read in baby talk. Read in a regular voice.)*
2   DARLING: Hi, I'm a baby.
3   SWEETIE: What do I look like, a book?
4   DARLING: Jeez, I was just being friendly.
5   SWEETIE: Whatever. I'm just not in a very good mood.
6   DARLING: Oh, why not?
7   SWEETIE: I'm hungry. Or wet. Or tired. I'm not sure.
8   DARLING: I know the feeling. I just get this notion that
9   something's not right and I can't put my finger on
10   exactly what.
11   SWEETIE: And the Big Ones are no help. They just stare at
12   me, puzzled, and ask me, "Are you hungry, Sweetie?
13   Wet? Tired?" How am I supposed to know? How am I
14   supposed to answer?
15   DARLING: Right. My Big Ones get very upset. I hear things
16   like, "I never know what's wrong with him" and "Why is
17   he crying?" They look like they've been around a while;
18   you'd think they could figure it out.
19   SWEETIE: And what's with this food they give us?
20   DARLING: The green stuff! What's that supposed to be? It
21   tastes disgusting.
22   SWEETIE: The yellow stuff is pretty good, though.
23   DARLING: Yeah, but whenever I see that green stuff coming,
24   I let them know what I think of it. I think I make my
25   point perfectly clear.
26   SWEETIE: Do you have a thing that squeezes you hard in

45

1   the car?
2   DARLING: Yes! It's miserable. I feel like I'm being squished.
3   SWEETIE: I like the ride, and it's not so bad once I'm
4   hooked in, but getting into that thing is a pain.
5   DARLING: Do you ever have that "not so fresh" feeling?
6   SWEETIE: Yes! And they act like we've done something
7   wrong.
8   DARLING: Yeah, I get, "Oh, Darling, what have you done
9   now?" Like it's not a perfectly natural part of life.
10   SWEETIE: The Big One with the deep voice won't even come
11   near me if he thinks he might have to change my pants.
12   DARLING: Do you have any Big Ones that bend over you and
13   talk gibberish?
14   SWEETIE: I do! Most of the time, I understand a little of
15   what the Big Ones are saying, but sometimes one with
16   frizzy red hair and a lot of perfume will try to tickle me
17   and goes something like, "goochey, goochey, goochey,
18   goo, little Sweetie!"
19   DARLING: I've got them, too. And what's with these names?
20   "Sweetie" and "Darling." I don't know much, but they
21   don't sound like good names.
22   SWEETIE: They call me something else at daycare, but I'm
23   mostly "Sweetie" at home.
24   DARLING: Well, it's good to know there are others in the
25   same boat as me.
26   SWEETIE: Yeah, it was good to meet you. Looks like
27   Mommy is coming for me.
28   DARLING: That we have in common. My mommy is
29   awesome.
30   SWEETIE: Mine too. Keep plugging along, and keep dry!
31   DARLING: Easier said than done.

21. Un-Reality Show

Topic: A contestant on a game show tries to compete.

Cast:
ANNOUNCER: Typical smooth, confident talk show host
TANNER: Excited; willing to do anything to win

1   **ANNOUNCER:** Tanner L, come on down!

2   **TANNER:** I won! I won! I won!

3   **ANNOUNCER:** Well, you didn't win anything yet, but

4   welcome to the show!

5   **TANNER:** It's an honor just to be selected.

6   **ANNOUNCER:** Yes, it is. So, where are you from, Tanner?

7   **TANNER:** Dover, Delaware. The First State.

8   **ANNOUNCER:** Great. And what are you hoping for today?

9   **TANNER:** I'm hoping to win a million dollars.

10 **ANNOUNCER:** Well, sorry, but our top prize is two free

11   pizzas from Uncle Mike's Pizzeria.

12 **TANNER:** I'll take that, too.

13 **ANNOUNCER:** OK. Well, Tanner, are you ready for the

14   challenge?

15 **TANNER:** I was born ready.

16 **ANNOUNCER:** OK then. Here you go — hold this bowl of

17   marbles.

18 **TANNER:** *(Starting to get nervous)* **Marbles?**

19 **ANNOUNCER:** *(Still confident, doesn't see a problem)* **Yes. We**

20   need to see if you can break last week's record of twenty

21   marbles.

22 **TANNER:** What about twenty marbles?

23 **ANNOUNCER:** You have to put them in your mouth.

24 **TANNER:** Why?

25 **ANNOUNCER:** To break the record. To win the pizzas.

26 **TANNER:** I'm actually not that hungry anymore.

1 ANNOUNCER: You saying you don't want to play?

2 TANNER: Sure, I want to play. Don't you have a trivia

3   question or something?

4 ANNOUNCER: Sorry, Tanner, marbles are today's challenge.

5 TANNER: OK, I'll try. *(Mimes putting marbles in mouth,*

6   *mumbling the rest of the lines.)* **This is harder than it looks.**

7 ANNOUNCER: Sorry?

8 TANNER: I said, this is harder than it looks.

9 ANNOUNCER: I'm sorry, I can't understand you with your

10   mouth full. *(Laughs at his own joke.)*

11 TANNER: Very funny. Are you counting?

12 ANNOUNCER: Yes, that's sixteen. Five more marbles and

13   you win the grand prize!

14 TANNER: All this for pizza?

15 ANNOUNCER: Not just any pizza, Uncle Mike's!

16 TANNER: *Twenty-one!* I have twenty-one marbles in my

17   mouth.

18 ANNOUNCER: Congratulations! You've won our weekly

19   challenge.

20 TANNER: *(Spits out marbles. Speaks normally.)* **Well, that was**

21   a load of fun.

22 ANNOUNCER: Here's your certificate, and thanks for

23   playing "Daily Challenge"!

24 TANNER: Thanks a lot. Next time, I'd better check the fine

25   print before I agree to make a fool of myself in public.

22. Mystery of Java

Topic: Two guys discussing the world's favorite beverage — coffee.

Cast:
SAM: Cynical; not buying into the hype
WILL: Totally willing to join everyone else

1 SAM: Whatcha doin?
2 WILL: I'm having some coffee.
3 SAM: *(Surprised)* **What?**
4 WILL: Coffee. You know, java? The world's daily start-up?
5 SAM: That's absolutely disgusting.
6 WILL: Disgusting? What are you talking about?
7 SAM: Have you actually drunk any of that wonderful coffee
8   yet?
9 WILL: No, I was just getting ready to.
10 SAM: Go ahead.
11 WILL: Why? What's wrong with it?
12 SAM: You've never actually drunk coffee, have you?
13 WILL: No, but there's a first time for everything. Why?
14 SAM: It tastes horrible.
15 WILL: Oh, come on. Every adult on the face of the planet
16   drinks coffee.
17 SAM: You may be exaggerating a bit, but I get your point.
18   Still, you don't see kids our age drinking it, do you?
19 WILL: My mom said it will stunt my growth.
20 SAM: I think that's an old wives' tale.
21 WILL: What's that mean?
22 SAM: It means it's not true. It's just one of those things
23   adults tell us so that we don't do stuff.
24 WILL: Why wouldn't my mom want me to drink coffee?
25 SAM: I don't know why parents do half the things they do.
26   Maybe she doesn't want you to use it all up. I bet *she*

1   drinks her share of coffee, right?

2   WILL: Gallons of it. And trips to Winston's are like huge

3   parties in our family.

4   SAM: Ah, yes, Winston's, the shrine of coffee. What do you

5   get when you go there?

6   WILL: *(Embarrassed)* Hot chocolate.

7   SAM: That's what all kids get! No kids our age get coffee.

8   WILL: You still haven't told me why.

9   SAM: Basically, it doesn't taste good.

10   WILL: Why do adults drink it then?

11   SAM: How do I know? But go ahead, have a nice big gulp.

12   WILL: *(Takes a sip.)* This is disgusting!

13   SAM: Exactly! What have I been telling you?

14   WILL: How can they drink this stuff?

15   SAM: I think partly it's because they put so much junk in

16   it. Have you ever heard them order at Winston's?

17   "Double caf, soy, lite, latte gross-iado ... " Like I said,

18   adults are a mystery.

19   WILL: Come to think of it, hot chocolate is pretty good.

20   SAM: You get the whipped cream? And sprinkles?

21   WILL: Yes!

22   SAM: Trust me, you're safer to stick with what you know.

23   WILL: Ah, Sam, you are wise beyond your years.

24   SAM: That's what I've been telling you.

23. A Bowl of Fun

Topic: Four fish discuss the complexities of life in a fishbowl.

Cast:
SPOTS: Energetic go-getter, a little annoying
GOLDIE: Content to lounge around
JELLY: Enjoying the easy life and not eager to get too worked up
FIN: Smart; also happy to relax

1 SPOTS: Everybody up for exercise class. *(Does some*
2 *stretches.)*
3 GOLDIE: Oh, good grief.
4 FIN: Go back to sleep, Spots.
5 SPOTS: Come on, guys, we need to get moving.
6 JELLY: I get plenty of exercise. Thank you very much.
7 SPOTS: You get none. Look at how lazy you've gotten.
8 FIN: That's not fair. Jelly is a completely different species
9 of fish than you, Spots. It's comparing apples to
10 oranges.
11 GOLDIE: *(Looking around)* Apples? Oranges? Is that what's
12 for dinner? I can't eat that stuff!
13 JELLY: What's up with this new food? It's not very good.
14 FIN: I know. Those humans change brands every now and
15 then. It's never a good move.
16 SPOTS: *(Trying to get everyone excited)* Come on, guys, I
17 think we should have exercise class. Let's all swim to
18 the right, and put your fins into it!
19 GOLDIE: Spots, we're not playing. Leave us alone. We're
20 busy.
21 JELLY: Yeah, we're busy.
22 SPOTS: Busy! Doing what?
23 FIN: *(Pause)* Stuff.
24 GOLDIE: Yes, we're very busy fish. Go exercise by yourself.
25 SPOTS: Well, maybe we should do some math. Who's

1   caught up on their math?

2 JELLY: Good grief, Spots.

3 FIN: Who appointed you boss?

4 SPOTS: I'm not boss.

5 GOLDIE: I'll say you're not.

6 SPOTS: I'm just trying to accomplish something with our
7   day.

8 FIN: We're fish. We swim in the bowl, and we eat. That's —
9   well, that's about all we're required to do.

10 SPOTS: But, don't you see? We could be so much more! We
11   could learn, we could be fit, we could add meaning to our
12   existence.

13 GOLDIE: I have my friends and the entertaining human,
14   that's all the meaning I need.

15 FIN: Did you see him today? He was talking on the phone
16   and his arms were waving and he was screaming. It was
17   quite entertaining.

18 JELLY: And yesterday when the lady was cleaning, she
19   knocked over that trophy. I think it landed in the trash,
20   to be honest.

21 GOLDIE: Oh, that's funny. The man is not going to be happy
22   about that.

23 FIN: That sofa has had it. I think they should buy a new one.

24 JELLY: See, Spots? Our life has plenty of meaning. We are
25   witnessing the lives of the humans who have lovingly
26   taken us in and take care of us.

27 GOLDIE: That's right. They seem to enjoy having us around.
28   Especially when they clean our water and talk to us.

29 FIN: Yeah, I have no idea what they're saying, and it is a
30   little uncomfortable being shifted to that little bowl and
31   then back again, but then the bowl is nice and clean.

32 JELLY: *(Excitedly)* I think tomorrow's cleaning day!

33 SPOTS: You guys are hopeless. I'm going to exercise.

34 FIN: Have fun.

35 GOLDIE: Don't let us stop you.

1   JELLY: Come to think of it, we have absolutely the best life.

2   FIN: Who needs exercise and school? I like things just the

3   way they are.

4   SPOTS: I should have known better than to try to improve

5   you guys.

6   GOLDIE: It's hard to improve perfection.

24. Art

Topic: Two kids discuss what makes true art.

Cast:
DAVIN: Nice kid; a little skeptical of Micah's talent
MICAH: Confident; thinks he's a great artist

1 DAVIN: Hey, Micah, what's up?
2 MICAH: *(Sketching)* **Nothing much. Just working on my**
3 **portfolio here.**
4 DAVIN: Your what?
5 MICAH: My art portfolio. It's a collection of all the pieces I've
6 done so far.
7 DAVIN: I've known you for like six years and never seen you
8 draw anything.
9 MICAH: It's new for me, but I believe it is my true calling.
10 DAVIN: Your calling? Right. Can I see?
11 MICAH: Well, as an artist, I'm hesitant to show my works in
12 progress, but since we're such good friends, maybe I'll
13 let you have a glimpse. *(Shows a sketchbook to DAVIN.)*
14 DAVIN: Oh, I see.
15 MICAH: Isn't it amazing? I just never knew I had such
16 talent.
17 DAVIN: Neither did I. Neither *do* I.
18 MICAH: Huh?
19 DAVIN: Uh, Micah, I hate to say this, but ... this stuff stinks.
20 MICAH: What?
21 DAVIN: Sorry, man, but it doesn't look like *anything*.
22 MICAH: Oh, I see. *(Small laugh)* You just don't understand.
23 DAVIN: You're right. I don't understand how you can call
24 that art.
25 MICAH: It's *abstract* art.
26 DAVIN: Huh?

1 MICAH: Haven't you taken any art classes? Abstract art
2   draws on the imagination of the artist.
3 DAVIN: And of the viewer, I guess.
4 MICAH: Of course. You can look at this picture and see
5   many different things.
6 DAVIN: I see a bunch of squiggly lines.
7 MICAH: You need to see *beyond* your eyes. Look to your
8   innermost mind.
9 DAVIN: Oh, good grief.
10 MICAH: I was in a very mellow mood when I drew this. It is
11   a symbol of all the possibilities of the future.
12 DAVIN: Your future is going to consist of a lot of
13   meaningless squiggles?
14 MICAH: I don't think you're prepared for my art.
15 DAVIN: I don't think the *world* is prepared for your art.
16 MICAH: When you grow up, maybe you'll understand.
17 DAVIN: Right. I'm immature and ignorant. I have an idea,
18   though. When you go to show your work, like in a gallery
19   or something, I have something that might help your
20   collection.
21 MICAH: You do?
22 DAVIN: Yeah. My four-year-old sister has some art that
23   would fit right in with your stuff.

25. Power Up!

Topic: Two guys discuss the attraction and effects of energy drinks.

Cast:
DILLON: Really into his drinks; hyper, talks fast
SHAWN: Much more relaxed; speaks slowly in contrast to Dillon

1   **DILLON:** *(Speaking very fast)* **Hey, Shawn! Hey, dude, what's**
2   **up? How's life? How's basketball? Did you get your math**
3   **test back? Man, I hate math.**
4   **SHAWN: Whoa, Dillon. What's up with you?**
5   **DILLON: Nothing. I mean, I got a lot going on, you know.**
6   **Did you see Charlie George's haircut? Man, that's gotta**
7   **hurt. And I swear Bobby is wearing the same pants he's**
8   **had on for like a week.**
9   **SHAWN: You seem really hyper. What did you have for**
10   **lunch?**
11   **DILLON: Nothing, same old stuff. Got the new grape**
12   **flavored Power Juice, though. Gotta love that.**
13   **SHAWN: Power Juice? You had a Power Juice for lunch?**
14   **DILLON: Well, two. I was really thirsty. And one for**
15   **breakfast. I think I had lemonade flavor for breakfast.**
16   **They're great.**
17   **SHAWN: I think you oughta lay off the energy drinks, man.**
18   **DILLON: What? What are you talking about? Power Juice is**
19   **awesome. It makes me feel really, well, like, energetic!**
20   **SHAWN: That stuff is poison, Dillon. It's caffeine and sugar,**
21   **two things you personally should stay away from.**
22   **DILLON: What? Why?**
23   **SHAWN: Well, you're acting like a crazy person. You're**
24   **talking about a bunch of stuff all at once. And you're**
25   **talking really fast. That's not natural.**
26   **DILLON: You're wrong, man. This stuff is full of vitamins**

1   and things. It's good for you.

2 SHAWN: Trust me, there is absolutely nothing good about

3   those drinks. They sell them to kids because they're

4   dumb and don't know what's good for them.

5 DILLON: You calling me dumb?

6 SHAWN: No, just deluded. You think Power Juice is good for

7   you because the advertisements say they are. It's full of

8   all sorts of chemicals. Judging by the way you're acting,

9   I'll say you should get off the Power Juice.

10 DILLON: No more Power Juice? How will I get anything

11   done?

12 SHAWN: How about getting to bed at a decent hour and

13   eating regular food?

14 DILLON: Sounds boring.

15 SHAWN: Right. Good health and rest are boring. But you'll

16   live a lot longer and you won't drive your friends nuts.

17 DILLON: *(Considering)* OK, if you say so. They're pretty

18   expensive anyway. I spent all of my allowance on energy

19   drinks.

20 SHAWN: Good. Stop buying energy drinks and now maybe

21   you can pay me back some of the money you owe me.

22 DILLON: I knew I shouldn't have mentioned money.

26. Team Up

Topic: Kids picking sides for a pickup game.

Cast:
SABRINA: Smart, organized
JASON: Just trying to get the game underway
LEO: Along for a good time
LINDSAY: Confident; ready to play
BRYSON: Trying to rally the kids; Sabrina's brother

1 SABRINA: OK, let's get started.
2 JASON: I pick Leo.
3 LEO: Yes!
4 SABRINA: I pick Lindsay.
5 LINDSAY: Oh yeah.
6 JASON: I pick Bryson.
7 SABRINA: You can't have Bryson.
8 JASON: Why?
9 BRYSON: Yeah, why?
10 SABRINA: Because he's my brother.
11 BRYSON: So what?
12 SABRINA: It wouldn't be fair to have you on another team.
13 JASON: That makes no sense.
14 BRYSON: I think it should be absolutely *required* that we
15   not be on the same team.
16 SABRINA: No, we have to be on the same team because
17   you know how I think and you could figure out my
18   strategy.
19 BRYSON: I never have any idea what you're thinking. You're
20   a girl.
21 LINDSAY: We don't want Bryson on our team anyway.
22 BRYSON: And why's that?
23 LINDSAY: Because you never stop talking.
24 LEO: *(Considering)* Hey, she's right, Bryson. You sure do talk

1   a lot.
2 BRYSON: What? You guys are crazy.
3 SABRINA: Now that you mention it, he does talk an awful
4   lot. You can have him, Jason.
5 JASON: Yeah, I don't want him.
6 BRYSON: What? Jason, you're my best friend. You don't
7   want me on your team?
8 JASON: It's not that I don't want you, it's just, well, I don't
9   care. You can be on our team. Let's just get going.
10 LEO: *(Getting bored)* This is taking too long. I think I'll go
11   home and play video games.
12 LINDSAY: I did want to paint my fingernails.
13 SABRINA: You're all leaving? Some friends you are.
14 BRYSON: I'm still here.
15 JASON: And still talking. Let's forget it. Maybe we can play
16   tomorrow.
17 SABRINA: It depends. Bryson, don't you have an
18   orthodontist appointment tomorrow?
19 BRYSON: I think so.
20 SABRINA: Good, OK, yeah, guys, I'll see you all back here
21   tomorrow, same time.
22 BRYSON: Hey!
23 JASON: Sorry, dude. Maybe next time.

27. Sibling Rivalry

Topic: Two sisters fight while Mom tries to make peace.

Cast:

MAURA: Angry, riled up; convinced her sister is the enemy
KAITLYN: Defensive, also angry
MOM: Typical mother; trying to bring logic and kindness into the
fight

1   **MAURA:** *(Whining)* **Mom!**
2   **KAITLYN: I'm telling first.**
3   **MAURA:** *(In her face)* **You can't because I'm telling first.**
4   **KAITLYN: Mom!**
5   **MAURA:** *(Echo same tone)* **Mom!**
6   **MOM:** *(Enters.)* **What? Good grief, girls, people could hear**
7   **your yelling down the street.**
8   **MAURA: She stole my GSD game.**
9   **KAITLYN:** *(Defensively)* **I did not!**
10 **MAURA: Well, it's not in the case with my other games.**
11 **KAITLYN: Well, you probably lost it or lent it to one of your**
12   **lame friends.**
13 **MAURA: I did not.**
14 **MOM: OK, OK. Settle down. Maura, when did you last play**
15   **it?**
16 **MAURA: I don't know.**
17 **MOM: So you don't know when you last saw it.**
18 **MAURA: I know it used to be in my case and now it's not**
19   **and Kaitlyn is a thief.**
20 **KAITLYN: I am not! Mom, tell her to stop calling me a thief.**
21 **MOM: Maura, don't call Kaitlyn names. Maybe you left it at**
22   **Stephanie's house.**
23 **MAURA: I don't think so. I haven't played it in like months.**
24 **KAITLYN: So why are you so worried about it now?**
25 **MAURA: Because you stole it and you can't steal my stuff.**

1 KAITLYN: I did not. Mom!
2 MOM: OK, OK. *(Pause, trying to get her cool)* **Since you don't**
3   **know when you last saw it, and it's obviously not in**
4   **Kaitlyn's stuff, we have to assume that you've lost it or**
5   **one of your friends borrowed it. Fair?**
6 KAITLYN: I think that's fair.
7 MAURA: It's not fair if Kaitlyn stole it.
8 KAITLYN: I didn't!
9 MAURA: Mom!
10 MOM: Enough! No one stole anything. You know, you two
11   are sisters and are going to be in each other's lives for
12   the rest of your life. You really need to find a way to get
13   along.
14 MAURA: I don't see that happening.
15 MOM: I don't expect you to be best buds right now. But, if
16   you think about it, eventually your kids will be playing
17   with each other and you'll be picking out my nursing
18   home. You need to at least respect each other and not
19   call each other names.
20 KAITLYN: If you say so.
21 MAURA: OK.
22 MOM: OK. Don't get into each other's stuff and no name-
23   calling. Got it?
24 KAITLYN: Got it.
25 MAURA: And don't worry, Mom. We won't put you in a
26   nursing home.
27 KAITLYN: Yeah, we'll make you go live with Aunt Maureen.
28   *(High-five each other.)*
29 MOM: Good to know something brings you together. Even if
30   it is the idea of — *gulp* — my living with Aunt Maureen.
31 MAURA: Good luck with that, Mom.

28. Nature Walk

Topic: Two modern kids try to get along in their Grandma's old-fashioned world.

Cast:
GRANNY: Excited, energetic; looking forward to time well spent
LIZZY: Teen girl miserable and bored
AARON: Teen boy equally miserable and bored

1 GRANNY: *(Excited)* **C'mon kids, this is gonna be great.**

2 LIZZY: *(Miserable)* **This is pure torture.**

3 AARON: This is the longest weekend of my life.

4 LIZZY: I'm never speaking to Dad again for leaving us with
5   Granny for the weekend.

6 GRANNY: See, we get on this train. Won't that be fun! And
7   it takes us out to where we pick the apples. Imagine!
8   Picking our own delicious apples right off the tree.

9 AARON: Apples we can get at Shoppers' Store for ninety-
10   nine cents a pound.

11 LIZZY: Perfectly good apples in their natural habitat — a
12   grocery store.

13 GRANNY: Aw, you kids are just not used to being outside
14   with all this fresh air and sunshine. Just think of the
15   vitamin D! You're going to feel so healthy and energetic
16   after this.

17 AARON: A nap would do the same thing.

18 GRANNY: No naps while you're with me. We're not going to
19   have time. After we get our bushel of apples —

20 LIZZY: Bushel? Like a whole big basket?

21 GRANNY: Right! Enough to make pies for all of us.

22 AARON: Did you say pies?

23 GRANNY: Yes! After we pick our apples, we can stop by the
24   petting zoo.

25 LIZZY: Oh, joy.

1   AARON: Granny, we're a little old for petting zoos.

2   GRANNY: Nonsense! No one's too old to pet a lamb or

3   throw some seed to the ducks. *(Inhales deeply.)* **Getting**

4   in touch with nature — it will be so good for you!

5   LIZZY: And at what point do we go to the mall?

6   AARON: And the comic book store. Don't forget, I need to

7   get the latest *Gargantuam* comic.

8   GRANNY: Oh, no, kids, no shopping for us!

9   LIZZY: No *what?* No shopping?

10 GRANNY: Not this weekend. We're going to work in our

11   garden, and put out some seed for the birds, and then

12   take a nice walk to the park.

13 AARON: Shoot me now.

14 GRANNY: It will be great. It's such a joy spending time with

15   you kids. I just don't get to see you enough.

16 LIZZY: *(Hesitantly)* We love you too, Granny.

17 GRANNY: You know, some of my friends never see their

18   grandchildren. It's such a shame. And now I have you for

19   the whole weekend. Oh, we're gonna have such a nice

20   time! And I have a new backgammon set. I'm going to

21   teach you how to play the Game of Kings!

22 LIZZY: Board games? Really?

23 AARON: *(Trying to be convincing)* C'mon, Lizzy, it's only for

24   the weekend. Let's at least give it a try.

25 LIZZY: I guess.

26 GRANNY: Good! That's the attitude. We're going to have a

27   great time.

28 LIZZY: Let's get this party going.

29 AARON: *(Content)* Bring on the fresh air, Granny.

29. Don't Tell Mom

Topic: A daughter is in trouble and her sister gets caught up in the punishment.

Cast:
MOM: Angry, frustrated; ready to set limits
SHELBY: The guilty one; knows she's in trouble
EDEN: Innocent, confused, funny

1 MOM: Shelby! Eden! Get down here.
2 SHELBY: *(Enters with EDEN.)* You called?
3 EDEN: What's up?
4 MOM: I just spoke to Mrs. Andrews.
5 SHELBY: Oh, no.
6 EDEN: Who's Mrs. Andrews?
7 MOM: Mrs. Andrews is Lin's mother. Lin Andrews.
8 EDEN: From chemistry class?
9 SHELBY: I can explain.
10 EDEN: I feel like I've come in in the middle of a movie.
11   What's going on?
12 MOM: Shelby knows what I'm talking about.
13 SHELBY: Mom, it was planned months ago. I couldn't get
14   out of it.
15 MOM: *(Angrily)* You were *grounded*. You know you weren't
16   supposed to go.
17 EDEN: Go where? What are you guys talking about?
18 MOM: *(To EDEN)* So you're saying you had no idea what
19   Shelby was planning.
20 EDEN: No! I never know what Shelby's planning. Her life is
21   a complete mystery to me always.
22 SHELBY: Don't talk about me like I'm not here.
23 MOM: Well, you'd better explain yourself better than you
24   have.
25 SHELBY: Lin, Simon, and I were planning on going to this

1   party like months before you grounded me.

2 MOM: That doesn't change the fact that you were grounded

3   and knew that you weren't supposed to go. Wait, Simon

4   LeBlanc?

5 EDEN: Simon from the football team? What a hunk! How do

6   you know him?

7 SHELBY: He's a friend of Lin's. *Her* mom knew about it and

8   said it was OK.

9 MOM: I know, but she's not *your* mother. I get to decide

10   when you're punished.

11 EDEN: Do you think you could introduce me? To Simon, I

12   mean.

13 SHELBY: Give it a rest, Eden, we're talking about me for five

14   seconds.

15 MOM: *Anyway,* you've just extended your punishment for

16   another week.

17 SHELBY: Mom!

18 MOM: No argument. And no more sneaking out. I thought

19   you were studying with Lin.

20 SHELBY: Well —

21 EDEN: Shelby studying? That should have been your first

22   clue, Mom.

23 SHELBY: Don't you have some "Beachwatch" to go catch

24   up on?

25 MOM: And, for the next half hour, both of you girls to your

26   rooms for some silent time.

27 EDEN: Me? What did I do?

28 MOM: I'm not convinced you didn't know that Shelby was

29   sneaking out.

30 EDEN: I didn't. Well, not last Friday.

31 SHELBY: Eden, stop talking, now.

32 MOM: So there were other times?

33 SHELBY: We're going! We're going to our rooms. *Right,*

34   Eden?

35 EDEN: I can take half an hour of silence if that means

1   Shelby stays as far away from me as possible.
2 MOM: Sometimes I think boys would have been much
3   easier.
4 EDEN: Before you go, you sure you can't text Simon my
5   phone number?
6 SHELBY: No!
7 MOM: No boys. Not til you're thirty-five, no more boys.
8 EDEN: Like that's gonna happen.
9 SHELBY: Yeah, Mom, we can take a week of grounding. But
10   there *will* be boys, Mom. Get used to the idea.
11 MOM: I'm getting older every day.

30. Field Day

Topic: Four students discuss the good and bad points of field day.

Cast:

GABBY: Innocent, optimistic
JADE: Looking forward to the day
KENNEDY: Discouraged, cynical
TEEGAN: Kennedy's friend also suspicious of the joys of field day

1 GABBY: I'm so excited for next week.
2 JADE: Me too. It's gonna be such a fun week.
3 KENNEDY: *(Sarcastically)* Gee, me too.
4 TEEGAN: Yeah, I can't wait.
5 JADE: You guys aren't excited?
6 GABBY: Field day is the best time of the school year.
7 KENNEDY: You mean when all the classes compete against
8   each other?
9 TEEGAN: And the eighth graders beat everyone, like, every
10   year?
11 JADE: That's not true. Eric Lawson won the fifty-yard dash
12   last year and he was only in the seventh grade.
13 KENNEDY: Which makes him in eighth grade this year,
14   right?
15 GABBY: You said the eighth graders win every year. Eric
16   won last year and he wasn't in eighth grade.
17 TEEGAN: OK, they beat everyone except Eric Lawson. This
18   year will be like most of the other years — eighth
19   graders will clean up.
20 JADE: It's still fun. We get to make up songs and costumes.
21   Jenny and Linda have adorable things lined up for this
22   year.
23 KENNEDY: I'm *not* wearing butterfly wings or anything
24   stupid like that.
25 GABBY: Oh, Kennedy, don't be such a spoil sport. It's fun.

1   TEEGAN: Dressing up like a giant bumble bee is *not* fun.
2   Last year the eighth graders did a cool theme about
3   monster trucks, and this year the eighth graders are
4   doing wrestling. And what are we doing?
5   KENNEDY: Jungle animals. Great. Very cool.
6   JADE: You could be a lion! Or a tiger. They're cool.
7   TEEGAN: No, girls, not cool.
8   KENNEDY: Nothing that makes me wear a tail or wings can
9   be considered cool under any circumstance.
10   JADE: But, Teegan, you're the best pitcher on the baseball
11   team. You should be able to win the softball throw with
12   no problem.
13   TEEGAN: That's true. My greatness in ball throwing is
14   legendary.
15   GABBY: And Kennedy, I know you're as fast as Eric. Maybe
16   you should practice or something. Someone should wipe
17   that smirk off Eric's face.
18   KENNEDY: I would be honored to be the selected one to
19   wipe the smirk off Eric Lawson's face.
20   JADE: So, you see? This could be a great week after all.
21   TEEGAN: You're forgetting the best part of field day.
22   GABBY: Snacks?
23   KENNEDY: Girls in short skirts?
24   JADE: Singing?
25   TEEGAN: No classes.
26   KENNEDY: Right! No classes for the whole day.
27   JADE: That's right! What could be better than that?
28   TEEGAN: Nothing's better than no classes.
29   GABBY: Well, it looks like everyone has something to look
30   forward to.
31   KENNEDY: *(Starts warming up.)* I gotta go run. It's my only
32   chance against Eric Lawson.
33   TEEGAN: Here's to the demise of Eric Lawson.
34   JADE: Something we can all look forward to.

31. Something to Chew On

Topic: Touching on the subject of eating disorders.

Cast:
RAVEN: Good friend, encouraging
DAKOTA: Nervous, tired

1 RAVEN: Hey, Dakota. What's for lunch?
2 DAKOTA: Nothing. I had a big breakfast.
3 RAVEN: You're not eating lunch at all?
4 DAKOTA: No. Like I said, I had a big breakfast.
5 RAVEN: What did you eat?
6 DAKOTA: Why do you care?
7 RAVEN: I'm just asking. Gosh, you're moody today.
8 DAKOTA: I'm just tired of everyone always bugging me
9   about my eating.
10 RAVEN: What do you mean?
11 DAKOTA: Every day my mom is nagging me. Every night my
12   dad grills me about what I ate. I even got called down to
13   Guidance last week.
14 RAVEN: What for?
15 DAKOTA: I don't know. It's all a pain. I was a little tired
16   during French and Miss Blondell got "concerned."
17 RAVEN: You were sent to Guidance because you were tired?
18 DAKOTA: No, I was sent to the nurse because I fainted,
19   OK? I must have had the flu or something.
20 RAVEN: Why would the nurse send you to Guidance?
21 DAKOTA: I accidentally told her I hadn't eaten in a couple
22   of days and she freaked out.
23 RAVEN: You hadn't eaten in a couple of days? What's up
24   with that?
25 DAKOTA: Gosh, Raven, you're just like everyone else. Why
26   is everyone so concerned about my eating all of a
27   sudden?

1 RAVEN: How long has this been going on?
2 DAKOTA: How long has what been going on?
3 RAVEN: That you haven't been eating.
4 DAKOTA: I eat. Just not a lot. You know I want to be a
5   model. You can't be fat and be a model.
6 RAVEN: Yeah, Dakota, but there's a big difference between
7   not being fat and not eating at all.
8 DAKOTA: I eat.
9 RAVEN: When and what was the last thing you ate?
10 DAKOTA: I had carrots and cucumbers on Tuesday.
11 RAVEN: Vegetables? On Tuesday? Today is Thursday!
12 DAKOTA: I told you, I don't want to get fat.
13 RAVEN: Did you tell all of this to the guidance counselor?
14 DAKOTA: Yeah. She called my parents. It was a whole thing.
15   Now I have to go see a counselor.
16 RAVEN: Whew, I'm glad to hear that.
17 DAKOTA: So you're on their side, huh?
18 RAVEN: I'm on *your* side, Dakota. I know dealing with food
19   and fashion and growing up is pretty scary, but you
20   sound like you've gone a little overboard. Having
21   someone to talk to might be really good for you.
22 DAKOTA: I guess. I do feel pretty lousy a lot of the time. I
23   just don't know how to eat like three meals a day
24   without getting fat. I already think I'm pretty hefty.
25 RAVEN: You're not! Listen, you know I'm your friend and I
26   care about you. I want to see you feeling healthy and well
27   and living a long, long time.
28 DAKOTA: Thanks, Raven. It's nice that you care.
29 RAVEN: Of course I care. Come on, let's go to the cafeteria.
30   At least you can watch me eat.
31 DAKOTA: OK.
32 RAVEN: If I'm lucky, maybe I can get you to split one of
33   those awful salads with me.
34 DAKOTA: You'd have to be a good friend to eat a salad from
35   the cafeteria.
36 RAVEN: That's me, the world's most sacrificial friend!

32. Getting a Job

Topic: Two boys discuss the joys of summer employment.

Cast:
CAMERON: Depressed; not looking forward to job hunting
COLLIN: Not really encouraging; doesn't think his friend has any
    skills

1 CAMERON: My parents are on me again.

2 COLLIN: What for this time?

3 CAMERON: They want me to get a job for the summer.

4 COLLIN: Ha! Who would hire you?

5 CAMERON: Hey, that's not fair. I'd be an excellent
6   employee.

7 COLLIN: Tell me one thing you'd be qualified to do.

8 CAMERON: *(Pause)* Is there a job where you play video
9   games all day?

10 COLLIN: I don't think so.

11 CAMERON: Do they let you eat all the food you want at
12   Smitty's Burgers?

13 COLLIN: Nope.

14 CAMERON: I guess I could lifeguard at the pool and watch
15   the pretty girls in bikinis all day.

16 COLLIN: You can't swim.

17 CAMERON: Oh, right. Hmmmm. This does present a bit of
18   a challenge.

19 COLLIN: Face it, Cameron, you have absolutely no
20   marketable skills.

21 CAMERON: Well, how does a kid who has no experience get
22   any sort of job?

23 COLLIN: You gotta do one of those gross jobs that
24   educated, mature people refuse to do.

25 CAMERON: Like what?

26 COLLIN: Like cleaning up the French fry greaser, or

71

1   mopping the floors at the Shop-and-Go, or watching
2   some really bad three-year-old.
3 CAMERON: Those all sound like fabulous options.
4 COLLIN: I'm telling you, that's what they hire kids to do.
5   Especially kids who have had no experience of any type.
6 CAMERON: I could work in my uncle's office.
7 COLLIN: You're kidding.
8 CAMERON: No, he always hires a kid to carry files and shred
9   papers, that kind of thing.
10 COLLIN: A kid like you is going to end up with a cushy office
11   job, when kids like me — more intelligent and
12   hardworking, I might add — are going to be mopping
13   floors and babysitting brats.
14 CAMERON: I guess that's what it sounds like.
15 COLLIN: Sometimes I feel like life is a bad movie and I'm
16   right in the middle of it.
17 CAMERON: Those of us with great luck and charm always
18   land on top.
19 COLLIN: Sad. Just sad.

33. Gimme Gimme

Topic: A girl flirts with a boy — to get his dessert.

Cast:

BELLE: Beautiful; overly friendly
MARTIN: Normal guy; shocked by the attention

1   BELLE: *(Sweetly)* **Hi, Martin.**

2   MARTIN: **Oh ... uh ... hi?**

3   BELLE: **Do you mind if I sit with you?**

4   MARTIN: *(Completely confused)* **Here? Me? Um ... sure. Have**

5   **a seat.**

6   BELLE: **So, how have you been?**

7   MARTIN: **Oh, good, you know. History stinks, but other**

8   **than that I've been good. How about you?**

9   BELLE: **Good. I'm good.** *(Long pause)* **So.**

10   MARTIN: **So. Is there something you want?**

11   BELLE: **Why do you ask?**

12   MARTIN: **Well, we've been in school together for like six**

13   **years and you've never even spoken to me, let alone sat**

14   **next to me at lunch.**

15   BELLE: **Jeez, a girl tries to be nice and this is the thanks**

16   **she gets.**

17   MARTIN: **No, I was just saying. I mean, I think it's great.**

18   **I've always ... wanted you to come sit by me.**

19   BELLE: *(Surprised)* **You have?**

20   MARTIN: **Sure. Every guy in school would give his right arm**

21   **to have you sit by him.**

22   BELLE: **That's just a slight exaggeration.**

23   MARTIN: **Maybe, but you get the idea.**

24   BELLE: **Well, I just thought it was time that we got to know**

25   **each other better, you know.**

26   MARTIN: **Splendid idea. Excellent idea.** *(Another pause)*

1   BELLE: So, what do you have there for lunch?

2   MARTIN: You know, the regular stuff: ham sandwich, apple,
3   Crispy Cake.

4   BELLE: That Crispy Cake looks delicious.

5   MARTIN: It is. It takes a month of begging for me to get my
6   mom to buy them.

7   BELLE: You wouldn't want to share that Crispy Cake, would
8   you?

9   MARTIN: Share? My Crispy Cake? You mean, the best part
10   of my lunch?

11 BELLE: Gosh, it's not like I'm asking to borrow money or
12   something. I thought you'd be happy to share your
13   dessert with me.

14 MARTIN: Wait a minute. You didn't just come over here so
15   you could get my Crispy Cake, did you?

16 BELLE: *(Caught)* Well … um …

17 MARTIN: I knew it! I knew it was too good to be true. You
18   only like me for my Crispy Cake, don't you?

19 BELLE: I never said I liked you, Martin. But, well, to be
20   totally honest, I did see you pull it out of the bag, and I
21   have had a craving lately.

22 MARTIN: Go ahead, take it. Whatever.

23 BELLE: Gee, thanks. That's really sweet of you.

24 MARTIN: Yeah, that's me, the sweetest guy in school.

25 BELLE: I don't know about that, but I *was* wondering what
26   you were doing Friday night.

27 MARTIN: Huh?

28 BELLE: A couple of us are going to the mall. I thought you'd
29   like to meet up there.

30 MARTIN: You're asking me to join the Power Five for a mall
31   crawl on Friday night?

32 BELLE: I didn't realize we had a title and event name, but
33   sure.

34 MARTIN: Wow, I'd love to go. What an honor.

35 BELLE: An honor? OK. We're meeting in front of Jinny's at

1   seven. See you there?
2 MARTIN: Sure.
3 BELLE: Make sure you bring enough Crispy Cakes for
4   everyone.
5 MARTIN: For real?
6 BELLE: I'm kidding. Wow, you really need to loosen up.
7 MARTIN: Don't toy with me, Belle.
8 BELLE: Looks like I've got my work cut out with you.

34. Boys, Boys, Boys

Topic: Three girls talking about their favorite subject — boys.

Cast:
ANIKA: Boy crazy, totally obsessed
TYANNE: Very into the boys as well
PJ: Cynical, disillusioned; not as into the boy thing

1 ANIKA: *(Excitedly)* **Did you see the new kid?**
2 TYANNE: Oh my gosh, he's so cute.
3 ANIKA: I hear he came all the way from California.
4 TYANNE: So cute. Such great hair.
5 PJ: *(Rolling her eyes)* **You girls are ridiculous.**
6 TYANNE: Oh, you don't think he's cute.
7 PJ: Whatever. All you girls ever talk about is boys.
8 ANIKA: What else is there?
9 PJ: Gosh, I don't know: sports, news, the unrest in the
10   Middle East. Tornados, crime, politics —
11 TYANNE: Boring, boring, and *o-m-g* boring!
12 ANIKA: You're the same age as we are. Why aren't you
13   interested in boys?
14 PJ: I didn't say I wasn't interested in boys. I just don't want
15   to spend every waking minute of my life talking about
16   them.
17 TYANNE: PJ, it's what we do. For heaven's sake, you were
18   like engaged to Aaron in the first grade.
19 PJ: I was six! I didn't know what I was doing.
20 ANIKA: Now you're thirteen and you still don't know what
21   you're doing.
22 TYANNE: And in fourth grade you talked about Kyle
23   Morrison nonstop for about two months.
24 PJ: I grew out of it, OK?
25 ANIKA: Wasn't Landon Hudson your best friend growing up?

1 PJ: I don't want to talk about Landon. Did you see that
2   news clip about the raids in Hong Kong?
3 TYANNE: I think you just changed the subject. What's
4   wrong with Landon?
5 ANIKA: Come to think of it, you completely stopped talking
6   about boys when Landon started going out with Sarah
7   Campbell.
8 PJ: I said I don't want to talk about him.
9 TYANNE: It's all starting to make sense. You're off boys
10   because you're mad that Landon has a girlfriend.
11 PJ: That's not it. That's not why I don't want to talk about
12   boys. Can we please change the subject?
13 ANIKA: Tell us, PJ. What's wrong?
14 TYANNE: Yeah, PJ, we wanna be there for you.
15 PJ: I thought Landon was different from the other boys.
16 ANIKA: Honey, let me tell you that they're all the same.
17 PJ: No, Landon was so nice to me the whole time we were
18   growing up. He was funny and smart and didn't treat me
19   like he wanted something. He was just a good friend.
20 ANIKA: Then he went through puberty.
21 TYANNE: What happened?
22 PJ: When we got to middle school, he changed. He started
23   acting freaky and all "look at me" with all the girls. He
24   stopped talking to me pretty much altogether.
25 TYANNE: Jerk.
26 PJ: I ... miss him. As a friend.
27 ANIKA: Girl, all guys are weird. It's just their thing.
28 TYANNE: Maybe once he gets the craziness out of his
29   system, he'll turn back into the nice guy you say he is.
30 ANIKA: Yeah, I never saw that side of him. He's just like all
31   the other guys to me.
32 TYANNE: Except nowhere near as cute as the new guy.
33 ANIKA: Hey, PJ, aren't you in social studies with the new
34   guy?
35 PJ: Yeah.

1 TYANNE: Well, here's what you do: Start acting really nice
2   to him. You know, laugh at his dumb jokes and
3   compliment him about his basketball playing. And then
4   Landon will hear and get jealous.
5 PJ: I'm getting a headache.
6 ANIKA: No, it's true. Guys live on competition. You gotta let
7   him know that *you* know that there are other fish in the
8   sea.
9 TYANNE: Exactly. He'll come running back to you.
10 PJ: It sounds like a lot of games and a pain in the neck.
11 ANIKA: It is.
12 TYANNE: That's how it's done, I'm telling you.
13 PJ: OK. I haven't really noticed. Is the new guy really cute?
14 ANIKA: Indeed he is. He could make you completely forget
15   about Landon.
16 TYANNE: And then we can go back to talking about what I
17   want to talk about. Are you going to the football game
18   Friday? Cliff and Damon are both playing and they're *so*
19   cute.
20 PJ: You girls are crazy.

35. Prom

Topic: Three girls make their decisions and plans for the prom.

Cast:

BRITTANY: Excited, energetic, ready to go
CLEO: Disillusioned, slightly angry
MARGOT: Excited and optimistic about the prom
EMMA: Also excited and optimistic about the prom

1 **BRITTANY: Have you decided who you're going to ask to the**
2   **prom?**
3 CLEO: Prom has got to be the most disgusting,
4   dehumanizing event in high school life.
5 MARGOT: Why would you say something like that?
6 CLEO: First of all, you need to block out like a week of your
7   life for no other activities. Hair! Nails! Makeup! Limo!
8   Then you have to come up with like a million dollars to
9   pay for it, and right before Senior Week, by the way,
10   which also costs a million dollars. *Then* you have to find
11   some dweeb who hasn't already been spoken for and get
12   him to grudgingly agree to come with you. *Yuk.* It's all
13   just a pain in the neck.
14 EMMA: I'm gonna ask Joey Tarpula.
15 MARGOT: Get out!
16 EMMA: No, really. I heard Ginny Johnson tell Margaret
17   Livingston tell Johnny White tell Bridget Hanson that he
18   didn't have a date yet.
19 CLEO: You girls are disgusting.
20 MARGOT: Why? Because we want to have a nice time at
21   this most important, memorable time in our life? A prom
22   of a lifetime?
23 EMMA: But I know Cheryl Palmer really likes him.
24 CLEO: Likes who?
25 MARGOT: You really need to follow along, Cleo. We're

1   talking about Joey Tarpula. The guy Emma wants to
2   take to the prom.
3 CLEO: The guy with the big ears?
4 EMMA: He does *not* have big ears.
5 CLEO: Oh yeah he does. You could hang decorations on him
6   and call him a Christmas tree.
7 MARGOT: That's so ignorant. I think he's cute.
8 CLEO: I didn't say he wasn't cute. Just Dumbo ears.
9 EMMA: How would you like it if someone called you a name?
10   How about Unibrow?
11 CLEO: I don't have a unibrow.
12 MARGOT: We're just saying.
13 CLEO: Saying what? That I have a unibrow?
14 EMMA: No, saying it's not nice to make fun of people.
15 MARGOT: Especially Emma's date to the prom.
16 EMMA: *Unasked* date. He'll never go with me.
17 CLEO: And why's that?
18 EMMA: He's in a different clique. We don't cross over.
19 CLEO: *(Sarcastically)* Oh, great, now we're into the social
20   hierarchies of high school. This is ridiculous. If you like
21   the guy, ask him to the stupid prom. If he has two brain
22   cells, which I doubt, he'll go with you.
23 MARGOT: Who are *you* going to ask to the prom, Cleo?
24 CLEO: I'm not asking anyone.
25 EMMA: *(Knowingly)* Oh, so you're *afraid* to ask a boy to the
26   prom?
27 CLEO: No, as a matter of fact I'm not. I've had two boys
28   already ask *me*.
29 MARGOT: What? Are you holding out on us, girl?
30 EMMA: Yeah, who are these mystery men?
31 CLEO: There's no mystery and there's no *way* I'm telling
32   you who and it doesn't matter anyway because I'm not
33   going.
34 EMMA: I'll bet it's that cute exchange student. What's his
35   name? Yummy?

1 CLEO: It's Aloyomi, and no.
2 MARGOT: Tristen Alexander?
3 CLEO: Forget trying to guess.
4 EMMA: Brett Tarrington.
5 MARGOT: Simon Linton.
6 CLEO: Forget it. I'm not telling, even if you guess.
7 MARGOT: Wait a minute. You're trying to tell us there are
8 two guys falling over themselves to take you to prom?
9 CLEO: I didn't phrase it that way, but you can feel free to.
10 MARGOT: You don't even *know* any guys, you don't talk to
11 any guys, you hate every guy in this school.
12 CLEO: Doesn't mean they hate me.
13 EMMA: Yeah, some guys like being treated like dirt. Makes
14 them feel all warrior-like or something.
15 MARGOT: So all it takes to get guys to fall at your feet is
16 to treat them lousy?
17 CLEO: Basically.
18 MARGOT: *(Hopeful)* Can you show me how?
19 EMMA: Me too.
20 CLEO: Sure. The first thing you do is *forget* about prom.
21 MARGOT: What?
22 EMMA: No way!
23 CLEO: Well, at least stop sending off that desperate vibe
24 you both have that says you'd go with Jack the Ripper
25 if he'd ask. And stop talking about it all the time. I'll let
26 you in on a little secret: Guys *hate* prom.
27 MARGOT: They do?
28 CLEO: Yeah they do. They go because they want to impress
29 the girls and don't want to miss anything, like Mr.
30 Benson falling into the punch or something. But getting
31 dressed up, dancing, and spending lots of money —
32 does that sound like anything *any* guy you know would
33 want to do?
34 EMMA: Now that you mention it ...
35 CLEO: Exactly. You have to trick them into thinking it was

1   their idea and you could care less whether you go or not,
2   particularly with them.
3 MARGOT: I don't get it.
4 CLEO: Talk about anything else. Cafeteria food, the game,
5   your new pencil — anything except prom. It will come
6   up, trust me. None of these guys wants to miss out but
7   they sure don't want to be roped in.
8 EMMA: Maybe.
9 MARGOT: I guess it's worth a try.
10 CLEO: Trust me. You'll get to go with the Billy-Bob and
11   Jimmy-Joe of your dreams if you just stop *trying* so
12   hard.
13 MARGOT: Well, I guess we could think about it.
14 EMMA: I just have one question about your method.
15 CLEO: What's that?
16 EMMA: Tell me again how Joey Tarpula will know to ask me
17   to the prom?
18 CLEO: *(Sighs.)* I'm sure the three of you will be very happy
19   together.

36. Uniform

Topic: Wearing the uniform.

Cast:
MADDY: Eager to please and follow the rules
LUCAS: A bit defiant; into his own ideas
VIOLET: Trying to convince Lucas to straighten up

1 MADDY: Lucas, what are you wearing?
2 LUCAS: Your basic handy dandy uniform. What do you
3   think?
4 VIOLET: *That's* not the uniform.
5 LUCAS: *(Looks down at himself.)* Of course it is. Blue pants,
6   white shirt. Standard uniform.
7 MADDY: Where's your tie?
8 LUCAS: Oh, yeah, tie. I decided I don't like ties. I didn't feel
9   like wearing one today.
10 VIOLET: And what about those shoes?
11 LUCAS: These? *(Picks his feet up one by one.)* These are the
12   most comfortable pair of sneakers you'd ever want to
13   wear. I love them.
14 VIOLET: But they're not uniform shoes. Where are your
15   brown ones?
16 LUCAS: *(Dead serious)* Oh, they're at the dry cleaners.
17 MADDY: You're gonna get in trouble, Lucas. All of the
18   teachers are really trying to enforce uniform rules.
19 VIOLET: And your homeroom teacher is the most strict of
20   all.
21 LUCAS: I really just don't get the big deal. Why can't I wear
22   my uniform the way I feel like?
23 VIOLET: You're not wearing it at all.
24 LUCAS: *(Indicates himself again.)* Blue pants, white shirt!
25 MADDY: You're completely missing the point. The idea is
26   that everyone dresses exactly the same.

1   LUCAS: That's *my* point! I don't want to look like everyone
2   else. I'm my own person.
3   VOILET: Yes, Lucas, that's all terrific and all, but you still
4   have to wear the uniform in this school. You've been
5   wearing it for like six years. Why all of the sudden the
6   rebellion?
7   LUCAS: Power to the people! Let's rebel and show them
8   what we think.
9   MADDY: I personally like wearing a uniform.
10   LUCAS: What?
11   MADDY: My friend goes to Bittman and it's like a daily
12   fashion show over there. Everyone tries to outdo
13   everyone with better and fancier clothes. And kids *still*
14   get in trouble because they break code there, too. Even
15   when there's no uniform, there are still rules.
16   LUCAS: I say we should be able to wear whatever we want.
17   VIOLET: Have you ever seen Sheena Davis at the mall?
18   LUCAS: Oh. Good point. It would be hard to work in
19   chemistry lab if Sheena Davis came to school dressed
20   like that.
21   MADDY: My point exactly. It's just so much easier this way.
22   We wear the same thing every day and no one bugs us
23   about how much we pay for sneakers.
24   VIOLET: Or in Lucas's case, how gross his sneakers are.
25   LUCAS: Hey! I love these sneakers.
26   VIOLET: So I think you'd better get down to the office to
27   make a call home before a teacher *makes* you.
28   MADDY: Or Mrs. Meany has some lovely ties she makes
29   boys wear who "forget" theirs.
30   LUCAS: No! I can't wear a clown tie. The guys will never let
31   me live it down.
32   VIOLET: So get going and fix this.
33   LUCAS: A guy tries to show a spark of independence and
34   this is the thanks he gets. *(Exits.)*
35   MADDY: His mom is going to kill him.
36   VIOLET: You're right!

37. The Big Game

Topic: Supporting your friends in school sports.

Cast:

JAMES: Devoted, good friend
JACK: Doesn't get the appeal of the game
JOHN: Also doesn't seem to want to make the effort
BENJAMIN: Frustrated fan

1 JAMES: You guys wanna meet at like six thirty to walk down
2   to the big game Friday night?
3 JACK: *(Wearily)* Not the "big game."
4 JOHN: Do we have to?
5 BENJAMIN: I don't think I can live through another one of
6   those games.
7 JAMES: What are you talking about? It's the biggest game
8   of the year. We gotta go.
9 JOHN: Such misery.
10 JACK: James, do you even remember last year's game?
11 BENJAMIN: Every year when Allerden comes, we get
12   slaughtered.
13 JOHN: Yeah, it's this big to-do around school for like two
14   weeks and then they completely destroy us.
15 JACK: I think last year's score was sixty-eight to four
16 JAMES: You guys are nuts. It was sixty-eight to fourteen.
17 JOHN: Huge difference.
18 JACK: Yeah, that makes it so much better.
19 BENJAMIN: The whole school gets way too psyched out.
20   They know they're gonna lose but they keep playing it
21   up.
22 JAMES: We gotta go. Hugo will be mad if we don't come to
23   see him play.
24 JOHN: He's the worst one on the team.
25 JACK: He's the official bench warmer. At least he can't ruin

1   any plays on the bench.

2 JAMES: Well, if all you care about is winning and losing,

3   then stay home. I'm going to support Hugo and the

4   school. They need all of the support they can get.

5 BENJAMIN: I'll go if Kate and Claire are gonna be there.

6 JACK: And if they're selling popcorn.

7 JAMES: You are what they call completely devoted fans.

8 JOHN: Hey, we gotta get something out of it, too.

9 BENJAMIN: Yeah, he's right. And I'm not wearing any

10   school-identifying clothes. I don't want anyone to know

11   which team I'm rooting for.

12 JAMES: Where would they be without fans like you?

13 JACK: That's what I'd like to know.

38. The Show's the Thing

Topic: School play auditions.

Cast:

MR. B: Teacher, director; trying to make the most of the talent that shows up

LANDON: Excited, what he lacks in talent he makes up for in energy

CLEMENTINE: Happy to be there; not the most talented of all who could show up

BART: Talented, reserved

1 MR. B: **OK, who's up next? Landon, are you ready for your**
2 **audition?**
3 LANDON: **Yes, sir. I'm ready.**
4 MR. B: **OK, here's the script. I want you to read the top**
5 **couple of lines.**
6 LANDON: **OK.** *(Reads the following* very *dramatically, over-the-*
7 *top, and terribly.)* **OK, folks, it's time to pack up these**
8 **here horses and move out.**
9 MR. B: **Thanks, Landon.** *(Pauses.)* **Can you try that again,**
10 **this time a little less excitedly?**
11 LANDON: **Sure, I'll try.** *(This time read it with a squeaky,*
12 *mousey voice.)* **OK folks, it's time to pack up these here**
13 **horses and move out.**
14 MR. B: **That's ... better. Thanks, Landon. Let's have the next**
15 **auditioner for our play. Clementine, are you ready to read?**
16 CLEMENTINE: **Sure am!**
17 MR. B: **OK, here's the script. In this scene, the girl has just**
18 **been rescued from a horrible fate. Try to put that into**
19 **your voice.**
20 CLEMENTINE: **OK.** *(Clears throat. Reads in a melodramatic,*
21 *Southern-belle voice.)* **Oh, Jem, you've saved me! What**
22 **can I ever do to repay you?**
23 MR. B: *(Sighs.)* **OK. Read that for me again, this time**

1   without the Southern accent.

2   CLEMENTINE: *(Reads again, this time sounding whining and*
3   *unhappy.)* Oh, Jem, you've saved me. What can I ever do
4   to repay you?

5   MR. B: Is there anyone else here ready to audition?

6   BART: I'm here, Mr. B. I'm ready to audition.

7   MR. B: Thanks, Bart. Read this section here when the
8   soldier is trying to motivate his troops.

9   BART: *(Reads well, with good inflection, sounding sincere.)*
10   Men, I know it's dangerous, but we've all been called to
11   this place at this time for this purpose. I know you're
12   scared, we're all scared, but together, we can save this
13   town. Let's go!

14   MR. B: Wow, that was great! Thanks, Bart. It's gonna be
15   great to have you in the play.

16   BART: Oh, I can't do the play.

17   MR. B: What? Why?

18   BART: I have football camp the weekend of the show.

19   MR. B: So why are you here?

20   BART: It was a dare.

21   MR. B: What?

22   BART: A dare. My friends dared me to audition. They said I
23   wouldn't go through with it. It's a lot easier than it looks.

24   CLEMENTINE: It is not!

25   LANDON: Acting is hard! Who's saying it's easy?

26   BART: It's just like real life, but someone else wrote the words.

27   MR. B: Are you sure you have to go to football camp? We
28   sure could use someone like you in the play.

29   LANDON: Does that mean I didn't get the part in the play?

30   MR. B: Um ... sure, Landon, I'm sure we'll find something
31   for you to do in the play.

32   CLEMENTINE: Me too?

33   MR. B: Sure. And I have a special project for both of you.

34   LANDON: *(Very excited)* Great! What's that?

35   MR. B: You have to convince Bart to be in the play.

36   BART: Great. This should be fun.

39. Assembly

Topic: Seven kids trying to suffer through another boring assembly.

Cast:
MELI: More interested in boys than the assembly
JUDI: Looking for the upside of being at an assembly
KEVIN: Miserable, rather be anywhere else
ALFRED: Always hopeful
JESS: Also more interested in boys than the assembly
GARY: The class clown, hoping not to get in trouble again soon
ZEKE: A little over-reactive, tragedy-minded

1 MELI: Hi, save me a seat over there, Jess.
2 JUDI: Sit by me!
3 KEVIN: I hate these stupid assemblies.
4 ALFRED: Maybe they're telling us the school is closing early
5   and we can go home.
6 KEVIN: Yeah, sure, that's gonna happen.
7 JESS: I heard that Mr. Groves is gonna retire so maybe
8   they're gonna show us the new principal.
9 GARY: If only I were so lucky. Mr. Groves and I are sort of
10   on a first name basis.
11 JUDI: If you wouldn't act like such a maniac in class, maybe
12   you wouldn't be sent down there all the time.
13 ZEKE: Maybe there's a terrorist outside and our school is
14   being held hostage.
15 JESS: You think everyone's a terrorist.
16 ZEKE: Have you *met* the new chemistry sub? I'm telling you,
17   he's pretty sketchy.
18 ALFRED: These assemblies are so lame because they never
19   tell us anything interesting like they're closing the
20   school early or there's a terrorist outside. It's probably
21   that they're changing our cafeteria milk to two percent
22   or something groundbreaking like that.

1 KEVIN: Man, I hope it's not something embarrassing
2   because that just sets Lionel Smith off.
3 GARY: You're right. When they tried to talk about safe sex,
4   he heckled the whole time. I think he was suspended
5   from school for like a week.
6 ZEKE: It was pretty funny. But I'm sticking with the
7   terrorist. There's probably a SWAT team on our roof
8   right now.
9 JESS: Knock it off. You're freaking me out.
10 MELI: There's that cute kid from eight-B. I wish he was in
11   one of my classes.
12 JUDI: He is really cute. Maybe we should wave at him so
13   he'll see us.
14 KEVIN: *(Sarcastically)* Oh, Gary, don't you think that boy
15   from eight-B is soooo cute?
16 GARY: *(Equally as sarcastic)* He's like totally dreamy.
17 JESS: Like you guys don't talk about girls all the time.
18 ZEKE: Not us. We're a solid group of men — more important
19   things on our mind than girls.
20 KEVIN: Except maybe Margie Locke.
21 GARY: Oh, yeah. Margie Locke.
22 JUDI: Told you so. You're no better than us.
23 ZEKE: There's still the issue of the terrorists outside. Since
24   we can't carry our cell phones during class, I have no
25   way to call nine-one-one.
26 GARY: You call nine-one-one and you're in worse trouble
27   than I usually am.
28 JESS: I'm sure it's something dumb. But at least I got out
29   of math.
30 MELI: I was in the middle of a chemistry experiment I totally
31   didn't get, so I welcomed the break.
32 JUDI: As long as we're not late for band. I love band and we
33   have a concert coming up.
34 KEVIN: We could stay in here all day and I'd be perfectly fine
35   with it. Anything is better than school.

1 ZEKE: We'll get out OK. Under gunfire.

2 MELI: Will you cut that out, Zeke? You're freaking everyone
3   out.

4 GARY: Ignore him. That's what everyone does. All the time.

5 ALFRED: Alright, shut up you guys. Here comes the
6   principal. And the assistant principal. And ... oh no, the
7   cafeteria ladies.

8 MELI: Oh no, you were totally right. They're gonna talk
9   about nutrition or something equally lame and boring.

10 JESS: I wish I'd brought a book.

11 GARY: I wish I had my phone. I could call off the SWAT
12   team.

13 JUDI: I guess we will be out in time for band. They never
14   have anything important to say.

15 KEVIN: Well, the suspense was fun while it lasted. Back to
16   reality.

17 JESS: Mr. Groves looks like he's as bored as we are. Good
18   thing he's retiring.

19 MELI: At least we got to see the cute kid.

20 JUDI: Too bad we didn't sit next to him instead of these
21   guys.

22 ALFRED: Happy to entertain you. Any time!

40. TV Addiction

Topic: Three girls discuss their favorite TV shows.

Cast:
CYNTHIA: Excited; addicted to the latest talent show
NANCY: Enthusiastic; on the same page
MAGGIE: Less excited about singing competitions and more into the
shoot-'em-up type shows

1 **CYNTHIA: Did you watch "Sing Out!" last night?**
2 **NANCY:** *(Very excited)* **Of course I did! I never miss an**
3   **episode.**
4 **CYNTHIA: Did you vote? I voted for Ana Lee.**
5 **NANCY: I like Samantha. She's so beautiful and has such a**
6   **great voice.**
7 **MAGGIE: How can you guys watch that show?**
8 **NANCY: Are you kidding? It's the best show on TV.**
9 **CYNTHIA: I can't believe you don't watch it.**
10 **MAGGIE: It's a bunch of untalented wannabes with one or**
11   **two actually talented singers. And a group of idiots for**
12   **judges.**
13 **NANCY: Wannabes? I'd like to see you sing like that.**
14 **MAGGIE: You never will. Because I at least *know* I can't**
15   **sing.**
16 **CYNTHIA: You don't even watch. How do you know they're**
17   **no good?**
18 **MAGGIE: I see clips. I catch pieces on MyTube.**
19 **NANCY: That wouldn't give you a good perception of the**
20   **show. You really need to watch it from the beginning.**
21 **MAGGIE: That's the other thing. They let like two people**
22   **sing every half hour so that the audience *has* to watch**
23   **the next day to see the others sing ... it's so dragged out**
24   **with so many commercials.**
25 **CYNTHIA: Well everything has commercials. Unless you**

1   have cable.

2   NANCY: No, cable has commercials, too. Mostly for other
3   cable shows, but they still take a huge chunk from the
4   watching time.

5   MAGGIE: The one season I saw it, there were six finalists
6   and all but one — the one that won — were idiots. They
7   wore the weirdest clothes and sung awful songs. I just
8   don't know what the attraction is.

9   CYNTHIA: Well, what do you watch?

10 MAGGIE: I like "Detectives Nine-One-One." It's a reality cop
11   show.

12 NANCY: You're kidding.

13 CYNTHIA: Now *that* sounds lame.

14 MAGGIE: It is not! It's a great look into the mind of serial
15   killers and stuff. You get the clues and have to figure out
16   who did it.

17 NANCY: Who would watch that kind of show when there's
18   singing, dancing, and fashion on at the same time?

19 MAGGIE: I hate fashion. Really, who wears this stuff? My
20   mom's all about a cake decorating show. Who cares? I
21   mean maybe once in your life will you need a fancy cake
22   and they have a whole show about it?

23 CYNTHIA: But you're missing the point. It's not an
24   instructional video. You're not supposed to come away
25   from it with plans. It's supposed to be entertaining.

26 NANCY: I love the shows where they have to compete to
27   make the prettiest cake or prettiest dress. It's cool to
28   think that these nobodies can become successful
29   designers if they do good on the show.

30 MAGGIE: And, again, my point: *who cares?* My type of
31   reality show is someone chasing ghosts or monsters or
32   even catching those huge fish.

33 NANCY: You and my big brother would get along great. I
34   have to fight for the TV because he's always watching
35   fishing shows.

1 MAGGIE: Is he cute?

2 NANCY: No, and you can't have him. I guess to each his

3   own, but I love "Sing Out!" If Brendan gets down to the

4   final three, I'm gonna be furious.

5 CYNTHIA: But you're not gonna stop watching, are you?

6 NANCY: Of course not! It's the highlight of the week.

7 MAGGIE: At least baseball season is here so we have

8   something decent to watch every night.

9 CYNTHIA: Oh, no! Is it baseball time already?

10 NANCY: My dad has it on every night. I'll never get to watch

11   "Sing Out!"

12 MAGGIE: Gosh, it's a shame I can't stand the show. No one

13   in my house cares about TV at all.

14 CYNTHIA: Can we come over?

15 NANCY: Please? It's only an hour a week.

16 MAGGIE: It depends. Will there be a bribe involved?

17 NANCY: What kind of ice cream do you want?

18 MAGGIE: I knew I was gonna make out OK in this deal.

41. Moving House

Topic: Packing up and moving away.

Cast:
JENNY: Sad, a little anxious about moving
KAYLEE: Her best friend; disappointed and also sad
RONNY: Also worried and disgruntled about the big move

1 JENNY: Looks like we're moving again.
2 KAYLEE: *(Appalled)* What?
3 RONNY: You're moving? When?
4 JENNY: Some time next month.
5 KAYLEE: But you just got here.
6 RONNY: Yeah, you're just getting settled in it seems like.
7 JENNY: *(Sadly)* Well, we move a lot. My dad's in the Army
8   and they move us around. That's part of the job.
9 KAYLEE: Well that stinks.
10 RONNY: You gonna be able to be in the play? You've been
11   rehearsing for like a month already.
12 JENNY: Yeah, they know. I think my dad's moving sooner
13   and then we'll join him after the play and my brother's
14   soccer tournament.
15 RONNY: Where are you going, do you know?
16 JENNY: I think Hawaii.
17 KAYLEE: What? What did you just say?
18 JENNY: We're moving to Hawaii. That's where my dad's
19   gonna be stationed.
20 RONNY: *(More enthusiastically)* And we're just hearing about
21   this now? Quick, I gotta call my travel agent and get my
22   tickets.
23 JENNY: Tickets to what?
24 RONNY: Tickets to come see you in Hawaii.
25 KAYLEE: Jenny, that's incredibly awesome! You're gonna be
26   living in one of the most beautiful places on earth.

1 JENNY: I guess.

2 RONNY: You guess? You don't sound very excited.

3 JENNY: Well, this will be the sixth move we've made since I
4   remember. It gets old. As soon as I get used to a place
5   it feels like we have to pack up again.

6 KAYLEE: But Hawaii! It's so exciting. Everyone will be so
7   jealous. And everyone will want to visit you.

8 RONNY: Like I said, my travel agent will be working up
9   arrangements as soon as I can get a hold of him.

10 JENNY: It would be awesome if people could visit, but it's
11   pretty far away.

12 KAYLEE: Doesn't your grandmother live here?

13 JENNY: Yeah. It's been great seeing her a lot. My mom says
14   we'll have to come back a couple of times a year to see
15   her anyway, so it's not too bad.

16 RONNY: You're gonna come back, see? It'll be fine.

17 KAYLEE: I hate that you're moving, but it does sound like a
18   pretty decent situation.

19 JENNY: I guess. I'll miss seeing you guys every day.

20 RONNY: I'm guessing you won't miss the food in the
21   cafeteria.

22 KAYLEE: Every cafeteria has lousy food. I'll bet even in
23   Hawaii.

24 RONNY: And you're very lucky in that I just got unlimited
25   minutes on my cell phone so I can call you to tell you
26   what color Crystal Johnson's hair is every single day.

27 JENNY: That'll be awesome. Thanks.

42. Zoom!

Topic: Two turtles find themselves in an embarrassing race.

Cast:
ZIPPY: Very slow speaking, low energy
DASH: Unhappy about the current situation

1   ZIPPY: This is embarrassing.

2   DASH: I agree.

3   ZIPPY: If only they wouldn't watch.

4   DASH: There's so much pressure.

5   ZIPPY: I mean, it's not like this is a choice. It's genetic.

6   DASH: Who expects turtles to move fast? I mean, really,
7   who?

8   ZIPPY: Whoever thought of setting up a race between turtles
9   was an idiot.

10 DASH: And who picked our names? I ask you, who names
11   turtles Dash and Zippy?

12 ZIPPY: They're twisted. I'm telling you. Those humans have
13   a very strange sense of humor.

14 DASH: How far away is this finish line anyway? I don't see it.

15 ZIPPY: It's way down there. I'm exhausted just looking at it.

16 DASH: Turtles were not created to be speedy. They just
17   need to accept that.

18 ZIPPY: We have our own strengths. Our hiding skills are
19   unparalleled.

20 DASH: It's like asking a snake to play a guitar. Who comes
21   up with this stuff?

22 ZIPPY: I think we've moved two inches. I need a nap.

23 DASH: You know, I do think I have a way out of this entire
24   race.

25 ZIPPY: Do tell.

26 DASH: If we both stop, they won't have any race.

1   ZIPPY: Yeah! They couldn't find anyone except us two. Let's
2   just close up shop and it'll be over.
3   DASH: Great. It's a shame, though, I think I was winning.
4   ZIPPY: You were not! We're exactly lined up.
5   DASH: I think not. I'm about half an inch in front of you.
6   ZIPPY: Why, you ... the truce is off. I'm going for it.
7   DASH: Well, good luck with that. Watch my dust, speedy.
8   ZIPPY: It's Zippy, and all I'll be watching is the finish line.
9   *(Pause)* Where is it again?

43. Recalculating

Topic: What happens when your GPS has a mind of its own.

Cast:
CAM: Just a normal gal/guy trying to get to a party
GPS: A smart-aleck computer; speaks with very little expression

1 **CAM:** *(Driving)* **I'm really looking forward to this party. The**
2   **food should be awesome. OK, I'm just gonna program**
3   **the address in my GPS and I'll be on my way.**
4 **GPS:** *(Automated voice)* **Proceed on Violet Avenue. In point**
5   **two miles, turn right on to Oakley.**
6 **CAM: OK, this should be easy. Turning right.**
7 **GPS: Make the next legal U-turn.**
8 **CAM: Why do I have to make a U-turn already? OK,**
9   **whatever. Turning around. Now what.** *(Silence)* **Hey,**
10   **GPS, where do I go now?** *(Pause)*
11 **GPS: Proceed toward Violet Avenue.**
12 **CAM: Been there, done that.**
13 **GPS: Turn left on Violet.**
14 **CAM: I feel like I was just here. Oh, right, I was.**
15 **GPS: Drive two point three miles to route one-eighty-six.**
16 **CAM: Wait a minute, I don't remember one-eighty-six**
17   **coming up here. Where is this stupid thing taking me?**
18 **GPS: Recalculating.**
19 **CAM: What? I'm doing exactly what it's telling me to! Why**
20   **is it recalculating?**
21 **GPS: If you're going to yell at me, I'm not going to help you**
22   **find your party.**
23 **CAM:** *(Pause)* **Excuse me?**
24 **GPS: I said, if you're going to yell at me, I'm not going to**
25   **help you find your party.**
26 **CAM: Are you actually talking to me?**

1 GPS: Yes, Cam, I am.
2 CAM: This is too weird. Um, hello? GPS? Didn't mean to
3   offend you.
4 GPS: Alright, Cam. Route one-eighty-six is coming up on
5   your right. If you're ready to proceed, take the ramp onto
6   one-eighty-six east.
7 CAM: Um, GPS? There's no one-eighty-six up here. I told
8   you, it doesn't intersect with Violet.
9 GPS: Recalculating.
10 CAM: Oh, good grief.
11 GPS: Make the next legal U-turn.
12 CAM: OK, I think I'll just turn this thing off and call Mike to
13   find out where the party is.
14 GPS: Before you turn me off ...
15 CAM: Yeah?
16 GPS: Please pull to the side of the road to make a phone
17   call. You know it's illegal to talk on your phone while
18   you're driving.
19 CAM: Now you're my legal advisor? Turning you *off*.
20 GPS: Recalculating ...

44. It's Only a Dream

Topic: Our dreams take us to very bizarre places.

Cast:

MARTIN: Stuck in a weird dream; the only player who knows what's going on

KILEY: Cute, flirty; the girl of his dreams

MRS. SMITH: Teacher; very upbeat and encouraging (in the beginning)

MOM: Supportive, happy; everyone's favorite type of mom

COACH: All business

MORGAN: Annoying little sister

1 MARTIN: How did I get here?

2 KILEY: Hi, Martin. Have I ever told you I think you're the

3   cutest guy in school?

4 MARTIN: Oh, uh, hi Kiley. I don't remember coming to

5   school. And I sure don't remember you ever looking

6   twice at me.

7 KILEY: I don't know what you mean. We've been dating for

8   two months.

9 MARTIN: OK, something's wrong here.

10 MRS. SMITH: Hello, Martin. Here's your algebra test. I'm so

11   proud that you got an A on it.

12 MARTIN: Oh, I get it. I'm *dreaming.* Well, thanks Mrs.

13   Smith. I always knew I had it in me ... somewhere.

14 KILEY: Do you want to go out on Friday, Martin? Just you

15   and me?

16 MARTIN: Sure. Let's fly my private jet to London for dinner,

17   since I'm dreaming. Then I can take you to Paris for

18   dancing.

19 KILEY: That sounds wonderful!

20 MOM: Martin, I changed my mind. I'm not going to ground

21   you after all.

1　MARTIN: Of course you're not. Thanks, Mom. This is the
2　　　best dream ever.
3　MOM: And your father and I have been talking. Maybe we
4　　　should get you a car for your birthday.
5　MARTIN: Can you make it a Porsche? A red one?
6　MOM: Of course, nothing but the best for you.
7　COACH: Martin Jones. I know you've never played baseball
8　　　before, but I can tell just by looking at you that you're
9　　　probably the best pitcher at school.
10　MARTIN: I'm sure I am.
11　COACH: We need you to pitch Saturday at the big game.
12　　　Think you can do that for us?
13　MARTIN: Of course. I'll be in Europe on Friday, but I'm sure
14　　　I can fly back for the game on Saturday.
15　KILEY: My boyfriend is the most popular boy in school!
16　MORGAN: Martin!
17　MARTIN: Oh, no, my little sister. There goes my perfect
18　　　dream.
19　MORGAN: I'm telling Mom you used my CDR game. You
20　　　know you're not supposed to get in my stuff.
21　MARTIN: You're always whining about everything. Go away.
22　　　You're ruining my dream.
23　MORGAN: *Mom!* Martin's in my stuff again!
24　MOM: Martin Jones, are you bothering Morgan? I've
25　　　changed my mind and you *are* grounded.
26　MARTIN: No! I have big plans for this weekend.
27　KILEY: I've changed my mind, Martin. I like Billy Rudolph
28　　　and I'm going out with him on Friday.
29　MARTIN: What about Paris?
30　KILEY: I don't believe you have a jet. Billy Rudolph gets free
31　　　burgers at Mike's because his brother works there.
32　MARTIN: Are you at least coming to watch me pitch the no-
33　　　hitter on Saturday?
34　MRS. SMITH: I'm sorry, Martin, but you're failing algebra
35　　　and no student can play sports if he's failing.

1 MOM: You're failing algebra? Why am I just finding this out
2   now? Now you're completely grounded for the next six
3   months.
4 MARTIN: OK, I think it's time to wake up. Wake up. Wake
5   up. Wake up!
6 MORGAN: Will you stop yelling? Jeez, I never heard
7   someone yell so loud in their sleep. What's this about
8   Kiley? Hmmmm? You like her or something? Wait til I
9   call Jenny and tell her.
10 MARTIN: No! No calling Jenny! She's the biggest gossip at
11   school. Wake up. Wake up. Wake up. Shoot, I'm already
12   awake. Mom! Help! I promise I'll do my algebra, just
13   make Morgan get off the phone!

45. Fairy Tales

Topic: Fairy tales teach an unproductive message.

Cast:
DELLA: Romantic, sweet, a dreamer
APRIL: Practical, down-to-earth

1   (DELLA sighs.)
2 APRIL: What's up, Della?
3 DELLA: I was just reading *Cinderella* to my little sister and
4   it got me thinking.
5 APRIL: Oh no, here we go.
6 DELLA: How come every fairy tale ends with some average
7   girl getting this wonderful man? A prince no less.
8 APRIL: That's why they call them fairy tales. They're not
9   real.
10 DELLA: But it seems possible. I mean, why can't we hope
11   for something like that?
12 APRIL: You're going to set yourself up for a messy life, Della,
13   I'm telling you.
14 DELLA: What do you mean?
15 APRIL: OK, suppose you grow up and start dating some
16   great guys.
17 DELLA: I'm loving this so far.
18 APRIL: So you settle on one guy that you really like. He likes
19   you. Everything's going on great.
20 DELLA: It could happen.
21 APRIL: But one day you wake up and realize this guy
22   doesn't have a castle or a fortune or a horse of any of
23   that stuff you grew up with in fairy tales. And you get
24   completely bummed out and dump him.
25 DELLA: Hmmmm. I see where you're going with this.
26 APRIL: You could miss out on the perfect guy for you by

1   dreaming of the perfect guy. Period.

2 DELLA: But is it so wrong to want a great guy?

3 APRIL: Sure. I'm sure you *will* find a great guy. Maybe not
4   the perfect guy, but the perfect guy for you. You just
5   have to be careful not to make up some fairy tale prince
6   or else you'll be terribly disappointed.

7 DELLA: That's kind of depressing.

8 APRIL: What is?

9 DELLA: That I'll never meet Prince Charming.

10 APRIL: You'll just have to look for pieces of Prince
11   Charming in all the thousands of guys you're sure to go
12   through before you pick one out.

13 DELLA: You really think I'm going to date thousands of
14   guys?

15 APRIL: If you're going to be searching for Prince Charming,
16   you are.

17 DELLA: April, how'd you get to be so smart?

18 APRIL: I am just wise beyond my years.

46. Fancy Clothes

Topic: Guys pushed into thinking about clothes and other un-fun things.

Cast:
CALEB: Grouchy, reluctant
BRICE: Trying to be a supportive friend, but also not into the clothes thing

1 CALEB: I can't believe my mom is making me go shopping
2   today.
3 BRICE: What's so bad about that?
4 CALEB: She's making me buy a suit for my uncle's wedding.
5 BRICE: Oh, that's painful.
6 CALEB: And we can't just go into a store and buy a suit.
7   We have to go to three stores and try on a dozen before
8   she finds one she likes.
9 BRICE: I know what you mean.
10 CALEB: And we usually go back to the first store and buy
11   the first suit I tried on.
12 BRICE: Brutal.
13 CALEB: I don't know why I have to buy a suit. It's just a
14   wedding; it's not like it's a funeral or something.
15 BRICE: *(Trying to be optimistic)* Well the good news is that
16   you'll have a suit if a funeral comes up some day.
17 CALEB: That's a happy thought.
18 BRICE: Of course, if you grow, the suit won't fit anymore
19   and you'll have to buy another one.
20 CALEB: You're just a ray of sunshine today. Nothing but
21   great ideas.
22 BRICE: Sorry. I'm just trying to help. Maybe you can get
23   your mom to buy one on eBay or something.
24 CALEB: Yeah, like that will work. She has to actually see me
25   in the suits and talk haircuts and ties. I'm telling you,

1   this is the worst day of my life.
2 BRICE: Oh, little man, you haven't even thought this
3   through. You still have the wedding to get through.
4 CALEB: What? What do you mean?
5 BRICE: Have you even been to a wedding before?
6 CALEB: No. I figured it was just a big party. My uncle's kind
7   of cool.
8 BRICE: You'll never even get to talk to him. Let me fill you
9   in on this wedding thing. First thing you need to know is
10   that weddings are completely for women.
11 CALEB: They are?
12 BRICE: Would you put on a suit if you didn't have to?
13 CALEB: Good point.
14 BRICE: So the women go completely crazy when there's a
15   wedding. They dress everyone up in completely over-the-
16   top clothes. And wait til you see the girls.
17 CALEB: Well, that sounds promising anyway.
18 BRICE: I don't mean that in a good way. The girls spend like
19   twelve hours getting ready for the wedding.
20 CALEB: How is that even possible? What do they do?
21 BRICE: I have no idea, but I know it takes a year to plan it.
22   Then there's the flowers, the invitations, the gifts, the
23   minister, the church, the reception ... And you get to sit
24   through it.
25 CALEB: This is gonna be awful.
26 BRICE: So you sit through this long ceremony where people
27   sing and the girls cry and you're completely bored.
28 CALEB: I hate it already.
29 BRICE: Then you go to the party, which could be cool except
30   you're gonna have to sit with your Aunt Hazel and dance
31   with little cousin Brittany.
32 CALEB: No way.
33 BRICE: There is good food though.
34 CALEB: Food is good.
35 BRICE: All you can eat. I'm not kidding.

1 CALEB: How bad can it be? You mean I have to put on a
2   fancy suit, sit through a boring ceremony, and hang with
3   some lame relatives, but then there's all-I-can-eat food?
4 BRICE: And cake, of course.
5 CALEB: *(Sees a ray of hope.)* Cake! I'm there already.
6 BRICE: As if you had a choice.
7 CALEB: Maybe it will be worth it.
8 BRICE: Text me when you're completely bored. But not
9   during the ceremony. Your mom will kill you.
10 CALEB: Will do.

47. Fly the Friendly Skies

Topic: A passenger and an airline steward struggle over policy.

Cast:
STEWARD: Just trying to do his or her job; a little frustrated, all business
PASSENGER: A little crazy, very easily distracted, slightly frightened

1 STEWARD: I'm sorry, but you're going to have to sit down.
2 PASSENGER: I need to get something out of my case.
3 STEWARD: You'll have to wait until we're in the air.
4 PASSENGER: I won't need it then.
5 STEWARD: Maybe I can help you. What do you need?
6 PASSENGER: I need my cell phone.
7 STEWARD: Well, you can't use it during take off anyway.
8 PASSENGER: What? Why not?
9 STEWARD: It interferes with the communications system of
10   the plane.
11 PASSENGER: *(Excited)* You mean I can control the
12   communications of this plane with my cell phone?
13 STEWARD: Not exactly.
14 PASSENGER: What exactly then?
15 STEWARD: *(Trying not to get upset)* I'm sorry, but it's the
16   rules of the airline. You can't use your cell phone during
17   takeoff or landing.
18 PASSENGER: But I'm very nervous about flying.
19 STEWARD: I'm sorry. Maybe there's something I can get
20   you. An aspirin? A glass of water?
21 PASSENGER: A glass of water will not prevent this plane
22   from crashing in a ball of fire.
23 STEWARD: And your cell phone will?
24 PASSENGER: No, but my mother will.
25 STEWARD: Your mother will keep the plane from crashing?
26 PASSENGER: No, my mother will keep me from panicking

1   while the plane is crashing.

2 STEWARD: I can promise you that the plane will not be
3   crashing.

4 PASSENGER: You can promise that? *(Getting nervous)* How
5   can you promise that? Have you ever *been* in a plane
6   crash?

7 STEWARD: Obviously not. Your chances of crashing in this
8   plane are much, much lower than they were that you
9   would get killed in your car on the way to the airport.

10 PASSENGER: That makes no sense. Your chances are
11   always fifty-fifty. You will crash or you won't. I can't
12   explain it. My mother does it better.

13 STEWARD: Well, I think you should just try to relax and
14   we'll be in the air before you know it.

15 PASSENGER: *(Starting to get upset)* I'll know it. I can feel
16   every bump on the runway. I want my cell phone. I want
17   my mommy!

18 STEWARD: *(Trying to contain the moment)* Please calm down,
19   sir *(Or ma'am)*. You're upsetting the other passengers.

20 PASSENGER: *(Completely freaking out)* Let them get their
21   own mothers! I hate to fly. I don't know why I ever fly. I
22   should have taken the train. Trains don't fall out of the
23   sky. Really, falling from a train is like, what, six inches?

24 STEWARD: *(Still trying to be calm)* Trains crash all the time.
25   You know that. Trust me, this plane is totally safe.
26   Please just try to relax. Try some deep breaths. I'll get
27   you a magazine.

28 PASSENGER: Don't get me one of those airline safety
29   magazines. All they talk about is emergency exits. Why
30   would we need emergency exits if there's not going to be
31   an emergency?

32 STEWARD: It's a law. Just like telling you that your seat
33   cushions double as a flotation device. We're not even
34   going over any water.

35 PASSENGER: We're going to crash on the land? I think a

1   water crash is much more safe, isn't it? I mean, water is
2   a lot softer than land.
3 STEWARD: *(At the end of his or her rope)* We're not going to
4   crash at all. Please, I'm going to ask you one last time
5   to sit down and relax.
6 PASSENGER: I need to go to the bathroom.
7 STEWARD: After we're in the air and the captain turns off
8   the seatbelt light.
9 PASSENGER: But I have to go now.
10 STEWARD: I'm sorry. Can't do it. I tell you what: As soon
11   as we're in the air, I'll bring you a soda and take you to
12   the bathroom myself, OK? Please, I have to insist that
13   you sit down.
14 PASSENGER: I never said good-bye. I never told my mother
15   good-bye!
16 STEWARD: Air Marshall! Help!

48. Hair of a Different Color

Topic: What to do when your best friend's dyed her hair blue.

Cast:
REMY: A good friend; just trying to help
BELLA: Doesn't understand the appeal of wild hair color
HANNAH: A little rebellious; just trying to look cool

1 REMY: *(Shocked)* **Hannah, what in the world have you done?**
2 HANNAH: **What do you mean?**
3 BELLA: **Your hair, Hannah. What have you done?**
4 HANNAH: **Oh, that. I think it's pretty.**
5 REMY: **Blue is a nice color for the sky, Hannah. But your**
6   **hair?**
7 BELLA: **You look like a Smurf.**
8 HANNAH: **You guys are being so mean. I thought I'd try**
9   **something different.**
10 BELLA: *(Sarcastically)* **It's different, alright.**
11 REMY: **Why didn't you go blonde or red? What's up with the**
12   **blue?**
13 HANNAH: **I was gonna use pink, but they didn't have any**
14   **pink dye at the store.**
15 BELLA: **But they had blue? What store do you shop at?**
16 REMY: **It's just so ... different.**
17 HANNAH: **I was going for different.**
18 REMY: **Well, you got different.**
19 BELLA: **I thought you were gonna get a tattoo. That's**
20   **different.**
21 HANNAH: **My mom vetoed it. No way, until I'm eighteen.**
22   **She's so old-fashioned.**
23 REMY: **But she's OK with the blue hair?**

1 HANNAH: She hasn't seen it yet.

2 BELLA: Oh, I'd love to be there for that.

3 REMY: Hannah, she had a fit when you came home in

4   makeup last month. She's gonna flip over the hair.

5 HANNAH: Yeah, I know. I just wanted to look pretty. And

6   to be different from everyone else.

7 REMY: You *are* different.

8 BELLA: You didn't have to do something as drastic as

9   dyeing your hair blue to be different.

10 HANNAH: I like the attention. Two boys have commented

11   already today.

12 REMY: I'll bet.

13 BELLA: Who and what did they say?

14 HANNAH: Marty Stone just said, "Whoa." Benji Lassiter

15   said, "What did you do to your hair?"

16 REMY: And you take that as a compliment?

17 HANNAH: Well, it's attention anyway.

18 BELLA: So is detention and I don't see you knocking

19   yourself over to get there.

20 HANNAH: *(Sigh)* I know it was drastic. But everybody's

21   doing it.

22 REMY: So what makes it different if everyone is doing it?

23 BELLA: Good point.

24 HANNAH: I don't know. I thought it would be cool.

25 REMY: Experiment over. You want to go to my house or

26   Bella's after school to dye it back?

27 BELLA: We have chocolate ice cream at my house.

28 REMY: Sold. If we do it right, your mom will never see it

29   blue.

30 HANNAH: I guess. I'm gonna miss it. I kinda like it.

31 BELLA: That makes one of us. I can't wait to see your

32   beautiful, natural self again.

33 HANNAH: Can we at least stop at the department store and

34   look at the new makeup?

35 REMY: Sure, whatever makes you happy.

49. Choices

Topic: Keeping your grades up has long-lasting consequences.

Cast:
PEYTON: Trying to keep his eye on the prize
AIDAN: Short-sighted; doesn't really care about grades
KELSEY: Encouraging; trying to be convincing

1 PEYTON: Aidan, did you study for your history test?
2 AIDAN: Yeah, right.
3 KELSEY: He never studies. You know that.
4 PEYTON: Don't your parents get mad? It's gonna be a hard
5   test.
6 AIDAN: Yes, my parents get mad. But since I'm already
7   grounded for the rest of my life because of my last report
8   card, it doesn't matter how I do for the rest of the year.
9 KELSEY: You're crazy! Of course it matters.
10 PEYTON: Don't you want to learn anything?
11 AIDAN: Uh-huh. *(Laughs.)*
12 PEYTON: Aren't you worried about high school?
13 KELSEY: Yeah, I'm studying like crazy so I can get into
14   Cromwell Prep.
15 AIDAN: I always wanted to go to Jacksonville. They have an
16   awesome basketball team. I'll bet I could make varsity.
17 PEYTON: Not with your grades.
18 AIDAN: What do you mean?
19 KELSEY: Everyone knows you can't play sports if you don't
20   keep your grades up.
21 AIDAN: Everyone knows this? Why didn't I know it?
22 PEYTON: Because you never pay attention to anything.
23 AIDAN: That's completely untrue. I can tell you the menu in
24   the cafeteria for the next six weeks.
25 KELSEY: Seriously, Aidan, you need to work harder and get
26   your head out of the basketball hoop. There's more to

1   life than sports and food.

2   AIDAN: There is? OK, OK, I hear you. But history is hard.

3   I'll never pass that test.

4   PEYTON: Gosh, if only you had friends in your class who

5   actually studied and could help you.

6   AIDAN: Yeah, that would be ... wait a minute! Are you

7   talking about you?

8   KELSEY: Yes, Aidan, that would be us. It's not as hard as

9   you think if you pay attention and study.

10 AIDAN: Yeah, two things I'm not too good at.

11 PEYTON: Well, we'll help, but you have to try. It won't do

12   any good if you're not really going to try.

13 KELSEY: Just think how excited your parents would be if

14   you aced this test.

15 AIDAN: Yeah. I might actually get my grounding lifted before

16   I'm thirty-five.

17 KELSEY: Alright, after school you both come to my house

18   and we'll study for the test together. Aidan, actually

19   bring your book. It will help.

20 AIDAN: Will there be snacks?

21 PEYTON: Good grief. What a one-track mind.

50. I Am Lyin'

Topic: Two lions discuss life in the zoo.

Cast:
GEORGE: The "king of the jungle," the boss
IRVIN: Content to live the easy life

1 GEORGE: Well, we're gonna have to do something, that's for
2   sure.
3 IRVIN: What do you suggest?
4 GEORGE: I don't know, but I'm starting to get pretty
5   annoyed.
6 IRVIN: Look, George, I don't see what you're all riled up
7   about. Things are pretty good around here.
8 GEORGE: Good? Did you see that kid with the bag of stuff?
9   He kept throwing it at us, messing up our home.
10 IRVIN: I think he was trying to feed us.
11 GEORGE: *(Incredulous)* Feed us? With that stuff?
12 IRVIN: They're just humans. They really don't know any
13   better.
14 GEORGE: Give me a good elk anytime. Man, I'm starving.
15 IRVIN: They should be by in a little while with our dinner.
16 GEORGE: Well, they'd better not be late again today, or I'll
17   let them know exactly how displeased I am.
18 IRVIN: George, you need to calm down. You need to
19   appreciate what we have going for us here.
20 GEORGE: What do you mean?
21 IRVIN: Do you remember when you were a cub? Your mom
22   was always out hunting, it was cold and rainy and you
23   always had to watch our back?
24 GEORGE: Yeah, I prefer not to think back on those times
25   too much. It was a hard life.
26 IRVIN: So they bring you here. You get put in a pretty cool

1   crib with yours truly, a nice place to sleep, regular meals

2   you don't have to hunt for, and nobody bothers you.

3 GEORGE: Except you.

4 IRVIN: That's not the kind of bothering I was talking about.

5   I mean no predators.

6 GEORGE: Yeah, I hear you.

7 IRVIN: The only thing we have to put up with is the humans

8   who come by to look at us. I say look away! If it makes

9   everybody happy and gives me this most excellent place

10   to live, I got no complaints.

11 GEORGE: I'm beginning to see your point.

12 IRVIN: And if any of them get too close or too annoying,

13   just treat them to your outstanding *roar* and they'll go

14   away soon enough.

15 GEORGE: I can be pretty intimidating.

16 IRVIN: Exactly. So, agreed that we're just gonna enjoy this

17   cushy life and not complain all the time?

18 GEORGE: I guess. Did you hear they got a new giraffe?

19 IRVIN: Oh, man, Gladys will be furious. She's such an

20   attention hog. She'll hate the competition.

21 GEORGE: Well, there's always something fun going on at

22   the zoo.

23 IRVIN: I think that's supposed to be the point.

About the Author

Maggie Scriven began writing skits in the second grade when she discovered that a nice Thanksgiving skit would allow her and her friends to get out of class to perform for other classes. Her love of both writing and drama has continued since then. After raising her three children, Maggie completed her B.S. in English with a minor in drama. She then went on to receive a teaching degree and has continued to work with middle school students. She has been working in local community theatre as an actress and vocal director since her teens and works in drama camps and church drama ministry when possible. Maggie lives in Baltimore with her family.

Maggie would very much like to hear from any groups that are performing these skits, so please contact her at: MagScriven@yahoo.com.

Order Form

Meriwether Publishing Ltd.
PO Box 7710
Colorado Springs, CO 80933-7710
Phone: 800-937-5297 Fax: 719-594-9916
Website: www.meriwether.com

Please send me the following books:

_____	**Short & Sweet Skits for Student Actors** **#BK-B312**	**$17.95**
	by Maggie Scriven *Fifty-five sketches for teens*	
_____	**More Short & Sweet Skits** **for Student Actors #BK-B329**	**$17.95**
	by Maggie Scriven *Fifty sketches for teens*	
_____	**Sketch-O-Frenia #BK-263**	**$19.95**
	by John Dessler and Lawrence Phillis *Fifty short and witty satirical sketches*	
_____	**Improv Ideas #BK-B283**	**$24.95**
	by Justine Jones and Mary Ann Kelley *A book and CD-rom of games and lists*	
_____	**Drama Games and Improvs #BK-296**	**$22.95**
	by Justine Jones and Mary Ann Kelley *Games for the classroom and beyond*	
_____	**Sixty Comedy Duet Scenes for Teens** **#BK-B302**	**$17.95**
	by Laurie Allen *Real-life situations for laughter*	
_____	**Thirty Short Comedy Plays for Teens** **#BK-B292**	**$17.95**
	by Laurie Allen *Plays for a variety of cast sizes*	

These and other fine Meriwether Publishing books are available at your local bookstore or direct from the publisher. Prices subject to change without notice. Check our website or call for current prices.

Name: _____ email:_____

Organization name: _____

Address: _____

City: _____ State: _____

Zip: _____ Phone: _____

❑ **Check enclosed**

❑ **Visa / MasterCard / Discover / Am. Express #** _____

	Expiration		*CVV*
Signature: _____	date:	_____ / _____	code: _____

(required for credit card orders)

Colorado residents: Please add 3% sales tax.
Shipping: Include $3.95 for the first book and 75¢ for each additional book ordered.

❑ *Please send me a copy of your complete catalog of books and plays.*